Oliver P. Williams

Chirexden & Wissahickon

Phila   1987

The Rhetorical Presidency

The
Rhetorical
Presidency

Jeffrey K. Tulis

Princeton University Press

Princeton, New Jersey

Published by Princeton University Press, 41 William Street,
Princeton, New Jersey 08540
In the United Kingdom: Princeton University Press, Guildford, Surrey

Library of Congress Cataloging in Publication Data will be
found on the last printed page of this book

ISBN 0-691-07751-7

This book has been composed in Linotron Times Roman

Clothbound editions of Princeton University Press books
are printed on acid-free paper, and binding materials are
chosen for strength and durability. Paperbacks, although satisfactory
for personal collections, are not usually suitable for library rebinding

Printed in the United States of America by Princeton University Press,
Princeton, New Jersey

TO MY MOTHER
AND THE MEMORY OF MY FATHER

CONTENTS

ACKNOWLEDGMENTS

My attempt to speak, all at once, to readers with diverse interests in American politics—political development, political behavior, or political thought—was nurtured by a number of outstanding scholars of the presidency whose own work sets a high standard for research in one or more of these fields. Benjamin I. Page saw the merit of trying to address diverse audiences and provided guidance on how to do so. Elmer Cornwell planted the seed of this study in my head several years before I "discovered" the topic. Fred I. Greenstein unstintingly provided helpful criticism and allowed me to draw upon the vast bibliography on American politics that he carries in his head. Whatever merit this book displays as a theoretical work derives from the wisdom of my teacher, Herbert J. Storing.

A number of colleagues at Princeton took time from their own work to read mine. My thanks to Walter F. Murphy, Ezra Suleiman, Jameson Doig, and Robert C. Tucker for their suggestions on early drafts of various chapters. I am grateful to Anne Norton and Sheldon Wolin for illuminating discussions of several of the issues I treat.

Numerous colleagues at other institutions offered critiques of the text, forums to try out some ideas, or the opportunity to read their own related work in progress. I would like to thank Larry Arnhart, Peri Arnold, John Burke, Joseph Cropsey, Juan De Pasquale, Robert Eden, Ester Fuchs, J. David Greenstone, Samuel Kernell, Carnes Lord, and Uday Mehta for their various kindnesses, and I would especially like to thank the referees for Princeton University Press, Theodore Lowi and Michael Nelson, for their thoughtful reports.

I indicate a number of specific debts in the footnotes, but I shall also mention here a number of individuals whose own work has considerably influenced mine: Sotirios A. Barber, Joseph M. Bessette, James W. Ceaser, William F. Harris II, Harvey C. Mansfield, Jr., Gary J. Schmitt, and Glen E. Thurow.

The opportunity to work with very capable graduate students at

Notre Dame and Princeton has been a special pleasure. I would like to thank particularly all those who served as teaching assistants in my course on the presidency. The diligence and insight of my research assistant, Ines Molinaro, greatly enhanced the book.

The American Council of Learned Societies and, through it, the National Endowment for the Humanities provided a fellowship that enabled me to write free from regular teaching responsibilities. Michael Francis, on behalf of the Department of Government at Notre Dame, provided support for research assistance on Chapter 5. The Princeton University Committee on Research in the Humanities and Social Sciences provided support for assistance on Chapter 3. This project builds upon earlier work on rhetoric, leadership, and constitutionalism conducted at the White Burkett Miller Center of Public Affairs, University of Virginia. I am especially grateful for the encouragement of the Center's first director, Frederick E. Nolting. I appreciate the good guidance provided by Princeton University Press's new director, Walter Lippincott, and by my editors, Gail Ullman, and Sherry Wert. Slightly different versions of some material in Chapters 2 and 5 appeared as "The Two Constitutional Presidencies," in *The Presidency and the Political System*, ed. Michael Nelson (Washington, D.C.: CQ Press, 1983). Permission from Congressional Quarterly, Inc. to incorporate this material is gratefully acknowledged.

My wife, Jean Ehrenberg, lent her talents as historian to Chapter 3, and as psychologist to the whole endeavor. My family's patience and care were indispensable to the book's completion.

The Rhetorical Presidency

· 1 ·

INTRODUCTION:
THE RHETORICAL PRESIDENCY

When President Carter gathered his advisers together at Camp David in the summer of 1979 for the so-called "domestic summit," he "channeled the discussions beyond the subjects of energy and economics to the larger question of the nature of the leadership he and his administration [were] providing." The president concluded that he had "fallen into the trap of being head of government," rather than the leader of the people he had promised to be. As he emerged from Camp David to give his highly publicized "crisis of confidence" speech, the *Washington Post*'s front page banner headline proclaimed: CARTER SEEKING ORATORY TO MOVE AN ENTIRE NATION.[1]

Carter's policies were opposed, and to some extent replaced, by his successor's. But his aspiration to leadership was not. President Reagan ended his first term heralded as a popular leader, a "great communicator," even by critics of his policies. Reagan has taken his case to the people at least once every week of his administration through radio and television addresses, continuing a populist cam-

[1] *Washington Post*, July 14, 15, 16, 1979, p. 1.

3

paign for conservative causes begun several decades before his election. Direct popular appeal has been the central element of a political strategy that has produced a stunning string of partisan successes, including budget cuts, tax reform, a large military build-up and accompanying social and diplomatic policies. Beneath the differing policies of Democrats and Republicans and varying abilities to secure partisan objectives lies a common understanding of the essence of the modern presidency—rhetorical leadership.

Since the presidencies of Theodore Roosevelt and Woodrow Wilson, popular or mass rhetoric has become a principal tool of presidential governance. Presidents regularly "go over the heads" of Congress to the people at large in support of legislation and other initiatives. More importantly, the doctrine that a president ought to be a popular leader has become an unquestioned premise of our political culture. Far from questioning popular leadership, intellectuals and columnists have embraced the concept and appear to be constantly calling for more or better leadership of popular opinion. Today it is taken for granted that presidents have a *duty* constantly to defend themselves publicly, to promote policy initiatives nationwide, and to inspirit the population. And for many, this presidential "function" is not one duty among many, but rather the heart of the presidency— its essential task.

The rhetorical presidency is not just a fact of institutional change, like the growth of the White House staff, or the changing career patterns of congressmen. It is a profound development in American politics. The promise of popular leadership is the core of dominant interpretations of our whole political order, because such leadership is offered as the antidote for "gridlock" in our pluralistic constitutional system, the cure for the sickness of "ungovernability." Bound up in the common opinion that presidents should be popular leaders is a larger understanding—of how our whole political system works, of the contemporary problems of governance that we face, and of how the polity ought to function.[2]

[2] See, for example, Richard Neustadt, "Presidential Leadership: The Clerk against the Preacher," in *Problems and Prospects of Presidential Leadership*, ed.

The rhetorical presidency and the understanding of American politics that it signifies are twentieth-century inventions and discoveries. Our pre-twentieth-century polity proscribed the rhetorical presidency as ardently as we prescribe it. Consider the attitude toward popular rhetoric captured a century ago by a newspaperman who provided a verbatim account of one of Abraham Lincoln's speeches and of audience reaction to it:

> And here, fellow citizens, I may remark that in every crowd through which I have passed of late some allusion has been made to the present distracted condition of the country. It is naturally expected that I should say something upon this subject, but to touch upon it at all would involve an elaborate discussion of a great many questions and circumstances, would require more time than I can at present command, and would perhaps, unnecessarily commit me upon matters which have not yet fully developed themselves. [Immense cheering, and cries of "good!" "that's right!"][3]

Lincoln refused to speak about an impending civil war and was applauded. It is hard to imagine a crowd cheering any instance of "stonewalling" today.[4] Prior to this century, presidents preferred written communications between the branches of government to oral addresses to "the people." The relatively few popular speeches that were made differed in character from today's addresses. Most were patriotic orations for ceremonial occasions, some raised constitutional issues, and several spoke to the conduct of war. Very few were

---

James S. Young (Lanham, Md.: University Press of America, 1982), 1–36; idem, *Presidential Power*, 3rd ed. (New York: John Wiley & Sons, 1980; orig. publ. 1960).

[3] "Speech at Pittsburgh, Pa., February 15, 1861," in *The Collected Works of Abraham Lincoln*, ed. Roy P. Basler, 9 vols. (New Brunswick, N.J.: Rutgers University Press, 1953–55), 4:210.

[4] When Carter cancelled his energy speech at the time of his "domestic summit," he was widely criticized in the press. One of his responses to that criticism was, of course, to give another speech, the so-called "moral malaise" address. When Reagan cancelled his 1986 State of the Union Address because of the space shuttle disaster, his decision was questioned by some reporters, and most importantly, he replaced that speech with another, a nationally televised memorial delivered just before, and repeated on, the network news programs.

domestic "policy speeches" of the sort so common now, and attempts to move the nation by moral suasion in the absence of war were almost unknown. Like our present practice, the nineteenth-century proscription of popular rhetoric rested on a larger understanding of how the whole polity functioned and how it ought to function, including conceptions of statesmanship and of the constitutional order alternative to those dominant in twentieth-century political culture. The modern rhetorical presidency marks a change in the American meaning of governance.

What are the larger views of the Presidency and the political system underlying the simple distaste for popular rhetoric in the nineteenth century and the common heralding of popular leadership today? Why did those perspectives change? How did they change? Do any elements of the old theory and structure of governance persist in the conduct of contemporary American politics? Most importantly, what have been the political consequences of the development of the modern rhetorical presidency? This book offers an account of this transformation of American politics, an interpretation of its meaning, and an argument for its significance.[5]

Transformation or Development?

To be sure, students of American politics know that twentieth-century presidents speak to "the people" more than their nineteenth-

---

[5] Of course, similar changes have occurred in other polities. (See Richard Rose and Ezra Suleiman, eds., *Presidents and Prime Ministers* [Washington, D.C.: American Enterprise Institute, 1980].) In this study, comparison is confined to the intra-American issue of change in national governing arrangements over two centuries. How similar developments actually are elsewhere, and whether those developments point to similar socio-political causes, will not be determined here. However, this study of a single country can be a useful starting point for comparisons between polities by offering a detailed articulation of a phenomenon thought to be similar elsewhere, and by generating several plausible hypotheses—including the possibility that others have imitated the American experience; or that they have responded to similar, though semi-autonomous, indigenous developments; or some combination of these. Finally, and most important, whatever the causes, analysis of the meaning and significance of political change here will apply elsewhere, to the extent that governing arrangements are truly similar.

century predecessors did. That is not news. But the extent and significance of the change has gone almost unnoticed. What I have called the rhetorical presidency is usually regarded as a logical development of the institution rather than a fundamental transformation of it. On this common and dominant view, the modern rhetorical presidency was writ small in the founder's original design. Like a child grown mature, the modern rhetorical presidency represents change, but change prefigured in the government's original form.

Political scientists have devoted considerable attention to other features of the modern executive that they regard as truly fundamental changes. These include the regular active initiation and supervision of a legislative program; the use of the veto to oppose legislation as a matter of partisan policy rather than of constitutional propriety; the development and "institutionalization" of a large White House staff; and the development and use of "unilateral" powers, such as executive agreements in place of treaties, or the withholding of documents from Congress under doctrines of "executive privilege." Most scholars trace these developments to Franklin Roosevelt's administration; some, lamenting the developments, trace the use of unilateral powers to Presidents Johnson and Nixon. All of these changes are viewed by many students of the presidency as constituting "metamorphoses" of the institution.[6]

The changes that concern political scientists today are important developments, and there is much to learn from their accounts of them. But they do not constitute metamorphoses of the institution, whereas the rhetorical presidency *does* represent a true transformation of the presidency. All of the allegedly fundamental changes are constituent features of Alexander Hamilton's theory of governance, and many of them found practical expression as well in nineteenth-century administrations. In fact, our first president, George Wash-

[6] For an overview of these claims see, Fred I. Greenstein, "Change and Continuity in the Modern Presidency," in *The New American Political System*, ed. Anthony King (Washington, D.C.: American Enterprise Institute, 1977). See also Arthur Schlesinger, Jr., *The Imperial Presidency* (Boston: Houghton Mifflin Co., 1973); Richard Neustadt, "The President at Mid-Century," *Law and Contemporary Problems* (Autumn 1956): 610–11.

ington—with Hamilton's guidance—fashioned a legislative program, used the veto for policy purposes, and exercised all of the unilateral powers that are allegedly new today.[7] The growth and institutionalization of the White House staff finds no practical counterpart in the nineteenth century, but the view of an administrative state that legitimizes its existence can be found, again, in Hamilton.[8] Here, indeed, is an example of the maturation of an institution, grown from an original structure that contained the political equivalent of a genetic code for subsequent development.[9] Again, this is

[7] Stephen J. Wayne, *The Legislative Presidency* (New York: Harper & Row, 1978), 13–14; Alexander Hamilton, James Madison, and John Jay, *The Federalist Papers* (New York: New American Library, 1961), nos. 69–77; Herbert J. Storing, "Introduction," in Charles C. Thatch, *The Creation of the Presidency 1775–1789* (Baltimore: Johns Hopkins University Press, 1969), vi; Edward Corwin, *The President: Office and Powers*, 4th ed. (New York: New York University Press, 1957); Louis Fisher, *Constitutional Conflicts between Congress and the President* (Princeton, N.J.: Princeton University Press, 1985), ch. 5; Gary J. Schmitt, "Executive Agreements and Separation of Powers" (Ph.D. dissertation, University of Chicago, 1980).

[8] Alexander Hamilton, "Defense of the Funding System," in *The Papers of Alexander Hamilton*, ed. Harold C. Syrett, 26 vols. (New York: Columbia University Press, 1969–1979), 19:3–50; Hamilton, "The Report on the Subject of Manufactures," in *Papers*, 10:230–40; Harvey Flaumenhaft, "Alexander Hamilton and the Foundation of Good Government," *Political Science Reviewer* (Fall 1976): 143–214. Herbert J. Storing, "The Problem of Big Government," in *A Nation of States*, ed. Robert Goldwin (New York: Rand McNally, 1964); Sotirios A. Barber, *On What the Constitution Means* (Baltimore: Johns Hopkins University Press, 1984). Cf. Theodore Lowi, *The Personal President* (Ithaca, N.Y.: Cornell University Press, 1985), ch. 2. An excellent critique of the common traditional/modern distinction in presidency research is offered by Stephen Skowronek, "Presidential Leadership and Political Time," in *The Presidency and the Political System*, ed. Michael Nelson (Washington, D.C.: CQ Press, 1984).

[9] Because spokesmen can be found on several sides of most questions that we might put to the founding generation, it is important to note that I am not interested in rearticulating all of the founders' states of mind or concrete intentions. Rather, I attempt to identify those founding arguments that offer the most coherent interpretation of the ratified arrangements. In short, I wish to identify and elaborate the most important founding arguments in order to explore the logic of the Constitution itself. For an excellent statement of this methodological point of view, see Barber, *Constitution*, esp. 11, 155–59. For the metaphor of the genetic code, I am indebted to Erwin Hargrove and Michael Nelson, *Presidents, Politics, and Policy* (Baltimore: Johns Hopkins University Press, 1984), ch. 2.

precisely the view that most presidential scholars wrongly hold about the development of the rhetorical presidency. But I shall show that the founding theory explicitly proscribed such development, and that nineteenth-century practice embodied that proscription.

All accounts of political change presuppose a systemic posture, a view of what constitutes the essential character of the polity. Without that presumption, one cannot distinguish the core elements of a political system from the peripheral aspects, nor can one distinguish enduring from transient qualities of the governing arrangements. While all accounts of political development and change presuppose a systemic posture, few contemporary studies begin from an explicit systemic perspective. One purpose of this book is to articulate a series of explicitly systemic perspectives with which to identify and assess change and development in the American presidency.[10]

Institutional Partisanship

The most influential tradition of scholarship on the American presidency is unprepared for the task of assessing systemic change and its implications. Most students of the presidency view the political system from the perspective of the presidency. I call this stance "institutional partisanship," because it takes the side of the presidency in the executive's contests with other institutions. Perhaps due to the common division of fields by institution among those who study American politics, this problem of perspective is not confined to presidency scholars. Students of Congress or the judiciary often assume the centrality of their institution in the drama of American pol-

---

[10] There is a renewed interest in systemic perspectives, although much of the best work concerns presidential selection rather than the governing phase. See especially James W. Ceaser, *Presidential Selection: Theory and Development* (Princeton, N.J.: Princeton University Press, 1979). Nelson W. Polsby writes, "I count myself as one of those who as a result of the Watergate era have undertaken to attend on a more or less regular basis to the state of the American political system as a whole." *Consequences of Party Reform* (New York: Oxford University Press, 1983), xi. Notable recent studies include Lowi, *The Personal President*; Bert Rockman, *The Leadership Question* (New York: Praeger, 1984); and Hargrove and Nelson, *Presidents, Politics, and Policy*.

itics. The problem is especially acute for students of the presidency, however, because Richard Neustadt's book *Presidential Power* has been so influential.

Neustadt views "the Presidency from over the President's shoulder, looking out and down with the perspective of *his* place." The central theme of his work is "personal power and its politics: what it is, how to get it, how to keep it, how to lose it." Neustadt's book has been studied by presidents as well as scholars. Because of its exceptional influence, a number of critics of the "imperial" presidencies of Johnson and Nixon laid some blame on Neustadt himself for giving intellectual support to dangerous arrogations of power in the White House. Yet it is striking how so many critics of Neustadt's theory continue to accept his fundamentally presidential perspective. For many critics of Neustadt, the most troublesome aspect of presidential arrogation of power was that it had made it harder for presidents to accomplish their objectives! It is as if Presidents Nixon and Johnson, together with Richard Neustadt, had betrayed their institution and its future occupants.[11]

Institutional partisanship is one of two intellectual legacies of Neustadt's *Presidential Power*. The other influential inheritance is Neustadt's claim that successful exercises of presidential power are the products of skillful bargains with other politicians in the Washington community. Bargaining is central to a successful presidency because formal authority promises presidents power that it cannot provide. The notion that presidents can secure compliance with their wishes by simply demanding it is misplaced, according to Neustadt, because presidential commands are never self-executing. Their efficacy depends upon artful wielding of informal power through bargaining—by showing other politicians that they will be helped, or at least not hurt, by doing what the president wants.

It is striking that presidential appeals to the public are not a component of political strategy as originally developed by Neustadt.

---

[11] Neustadt, *Presidential Power* (see both the preface to the original edition and the preface to the 1980 edition); Schlesinger, *The Imperial Presidency*; Thomas Cronin, *The State of the Presidency*, 2nd ed. (Boston: Little, Brown & Co., 1980).

Samuel Kernell wonders why a book that purported to be a strategic manual for presidents failed to entertain the possibility of direct and dramatic applications of popular pressure.[12] He suggests the answer to this question to be the deep incompatibility of popular rhetoric and bargaining as political tactics. "Going public" subverts the logic of bargaining as a political strategy, and, according to Kernell, it undermines the pluralist premises upon which that strategy is built.

> Practiced in a dedicated way [going public] can threaten to displace bargaining . . . it fails to extend benefits for compliance, but freely imposes costs for noncompliance. . . . Going public is more akin to force than to bargaining . . . it makes subsequent compromise with other politicians difficult.[13]

Kernell's insight and the criticism that it generates are helpful. The rise of the rhetorical presidency reveals important inadequacies in previous strategic analyses. But an improved rendering of Neustadt's theory can survive this sort of attack upon its original formulation. This is because Neustadt's second legacy—the president as bargainer—is subservient to the first—the scholar as institutional partisan. The skillful use of popular rhetoric can be integrated into a bargaining perspective if one explores the conditions under which such appeals strengthen, weaken, or substitute for traditional exchange re-

[12] Samuel Kernell, *Going Public: New Strategies of Presidential Leadership* (Washington, D.C.: CQ Press, 1986), ch. 1; Neustadt, *Presidential Power*, 36; Joseph M. Bessette and Jeffrey Tulis, "The Constitution, Politics, and the Presidency," in *The Presidency in the Constitutional Order*, ed. Bessette and Tulis (Baton Rouge and London: Louisiana State University Press, 1981), 4–5; Harvey C. Mansfield, Jr., "The Ambivalence of Executive Power," in Bessette and Tulis, *The Presidency*, 319–22. For useful defenses of "command" and critiques of Neustadt's reliance upon bargaining, see Peter Sperlich, "Bargaining and Overload: An Essay on *Presidential Power*," in *The Presidency*, ed. Aaron Wildavsky (Boston: Little, Brown & Co., 1969); and see especially Richard Pious, *The American Presidency* (New York: Basic Books, 1979).

[13] Kernell, *Going Public*, ch. 1 (pp. 3–4); "[Noted pluralist Nelson] Polsby makes the same point when he says that congressmen may 'find themselves ill disposed toward a president who prefers to deal indirectly with them [by going public] through what they may interpret as *coercion* rather than face-to-face in the spirit of mutual accommodation.' " Ibid.

lations. Indeed, this is what Kernell does. More significantly, Neustadt is doing it himself. He has altered his strategic account in subsequent editions of his book in order to accommodate public appeals. The strategic use of the "bully pulpit" is a prominent theme of Neustadt's recent writing, in which he urges presidents to "keep trying to play in Peoria."[14]

Despite informed criticism, Richard Neustadt's study continues to set the categories of understanding for students of the presidency because institutional partisanship is so important, yet so little noticed. The touchstone of almost all analyses of the presidency today is presidential "effectiveness," understood as the long-term ability to accomplish whatever objectives presidents might have.

By contrast, in this book I place instances of presidential rhetoric within a larger context of changing conceptions of the political order. Presidential strategy is subordinated to a concern for illuminating some of the multiple and contradictory requisites of republican governance. Without preventing discussion of the strategic utility of rhetorical appeals for presidents' objectives, I explore the effect presidents' rhetorical practices have upon other aspects of the political system, such as the process of congressional deliberation. A systemic perspective also permits one to probe the various ways our political system should foster or constrain leadership. Most importantly, to look at American politics from the perspective of the polity rather than the presidency allows one to see the dilemmas that attend the constitution of executive power in a republican regime. From this perspective, the development of the rhetorical presidency does not appear to be an unqualified blessing as most scholars, citizens, and politicians assume, but rather a political development whose enor-

[14] Neustadt, *Presidential Power*, part 2; and idem, "Presidential Leadership: The Clerk against the Preacher," 33. The classic analysis in this tradition is still Elmer Cornwell, *Presidential Leadership of Public Opinion* (Bloomington: Indiana University Press, 1965). See also Michael Baruch Grossman and Martha Joynt Kumar, *Portraying the President* (Baltimore: Johns Hopkins University Press, 1981); and George C. Edwards III, *The Public Presidency* (New York: St. Martin's Press, 1983).

mous political promise has been accompanied by considerable systemic costs.

Reason and Rhetoric as Cause

The rhetorical presidency may have been generally ignored as an object of concern not only because it has become so familiar and comfortably democratic, but also because it is hard to believe that mere rhetoric could be of consequence to the development of American political institutions. Would it not be wiser, one might wonder, to regard rhetoric as, at best, a symptom of some phenomenon more worthy of our attention? Perhaps our presidents operate differently today than they did a century ago because the country is very different. For example, political parties have disintegrated, and television, unknown to the founders, has simultaneously opened up opportunities for and brought burdens to the modern presidency. Twentieth-century rhetoric may simply reflect these sorts of political developments.

This kind of objection to a focus upon the rhetorical presidency is misplaced, but it contains a kernel of truth. Political rhetoric is reflective of something more fundamental. But that more fundamental phenomenon is intimately bound up with rhetoric itself; it is the idea or set of ideas that legitimizes political practice. I examine the full array of nineteenth- and twentieth-century rhetorical practices as reflections *and* elaborations of underlying doctrines of governance. These doctrines or systemic understandings are the primary object of inquiry, and presidential rhetoric is their most visible practical manifestation. I will devote considerable attention to description of nineteenth- and twentieth-century rhetorical practices because those practices reveal the fact and consequence of basic change in the understanding of the place of the presidency in the political order.

The relation between fundamental doctrines of governance and presidential rhetoric is more complex than simple cause and effect because rhetoric is not only the result of various ideas, but also the medium for their expression. Rhetorical practice is not merely a variable, it is also an amplification or vulgarization of the ideas that produce it. Political rhetoric is, simultaneously, a practical result of basic doctrines of governance, and an avenue to the meaning of alternative constitutional understandings. The political meaning and consequence of those understandings is the central subject of this book.[15]

To indicate the importance of these underlying doctrines, consider the hypothetical objection again. The objection is misplaced, I argue, because it concerns rhetoric rather than the larger political frame that rhetoric expresses and reveals. Perhaps, our critic might reply, this larger frame itself is really a symptom of a more fundamental phenomenon.

One might argue, for example, that the "underlying root cause of" the new understandings of leadership is the "decay of political parties."[16] Presidents now need to build their own campaign organizations and to regularly appeal to "the people" for at least two years in order to secure nomination, let alone election. Perhaps the selection system is the chief determinant of modern understandings of governance.

It is true that modern presidents are schooled in contemporary rhetorical techniques before they reach office, and that recent presidents have tended to understand governing as a continuation and reduplication of campaigning. This is an important development in American politics.[17] But to treat the decay of political parties as the "root cause" of plebiscitary leadership is to not look deep enough. A number of students of the party system have shown that the transformation of political parties can best be understood as a result of changing

[15] The analysis of political meaning is especially important and requires an interpretive approach that goes beyond the identification of causal chains. See Clifford Geertz, *Local Knowledge* (New York: Basic Books, 1985); Lowi, *The Personal President*, 80; and Jeffrey K. Tulis, "The Interpretable Presidency," in *The Presidency and the Political System*, ed. Michael Nelson, 2nd ed. (Washington, D.C.: CQ Press, 1987).

[16] Kernell, *Going Public*, ch. 1.

[17] Jeff Fishel, *Presidents and Promises* (Washington, D.C.: CQ Press, 1985).

ideas that legitimate the parties' place in our political system.[18] The call for plebiscitary leadership preceded modern party reform and eventually legitimated that change. There is a very real sense in which plebiscitary leadership—that is, the ideas that this term signifies—caused party decay. Finally, party reform was concomitant with the rise of the rhetorical presidency, a result of some of the same doctrinal developments examined in this book.[19]

Still, the treatment of ideas as semi-autonomous factors in political development strikes many as naive. Perhaps, a sophisticated social scientist might suggest, technological change (such as television) drives doctrinal change. I do not deny that television has an independent effect on the character of presidential rhetoric (and I discuss some of these independent effects in Chapter 7); but the use of television for leadership purposes required prior legitimation through some set of ideas. Before presidents could appear on television, or radio, it had to be legitimate for them to do so. In fact, these particular technologies were usable before they were politically employed. They were available for exploitation but did not cause it. This idea is not as new nor as odd as it might first appear. Twenty-five years ago, Stanley Kelley provided an account of changing tactics in political campaigns, including "dirty" tactics. Kelley found that the use of "dirty" tactics required not only technical capability, but also a change in ethic, the advent of an accepting disposition on the part of the voting public. Prior to a doctrinal development legitimizing dirty tactics (making them no longer dirty), they could not be profitably employed.[20] So too with the modern technologies that attend the rhetorical presidency.

The greatest difficulty that faces one who would give great weight to the technical development of the mass media as determinant of the

[18] Richard Hofstadter, *The Idea of a Party System* (Berkeley: University of California Press, 1972); Ceaser, *Presidential Selection*.

[19] This point is made at greater length in James Ceaser, Glen Thurow, Jeffrey Tulis, and Joseph M. Bessette, "The Rise of the Rhetorical Presidency," in *Rethinking the Presidency*, ed. Thomas Cronin (Boston: Little, Brown & Co., 1982).

[20] Stanley Kelley Jr., *Political Campaigning: Problems in Creating an Informed Electorate* (Washington, D.C.: Brookings Institution, 1960), 152.

rhetorical presidency is the fact that presidents had much less technical difficulty in going to "the people" in the past than one might think. Although presidents made relatively few popular addresses in the nineteenth century compared to presidents in our century, taken together they did give a considerable number of speeches—about one thousand of them. I discuss these speeches in Chapter 3. Here I merely note that this rhetoric was well covered in newspaper accounts and widely circulated in pamphlet form. Of course, these speeches looked very different from speeches today and performed very different political functions—that is one of my central claims. Presidents could have made speeches that looked very similar to those made today, but they did not. They spoke and acted very differently than they could have done within the limits of available technology. The differences between nineteenth- and twentieth-century political rhetoric do not depend upon the development of the modern mass media, though contemporary presidential rhetoric is certainly reinforced by requirements of modern television. Rather, the differences depend essentially upon the very phenomena that they reveal—the changing conceptions of leadership and the place of these conceptions in our political order.

Although presidents faced few technical difficulties in "going public" in the nineteenth century, they did face enormous political difficulties, if they attempted to mount a policy-oriented campaign like those so common today. In Chapter 3, I discuss the effort of one nineteenth-century president who did attempt such a campaign. Andrew Johnson faced no important technical difficulty in going public to pressure Congress to support his reconstruction policies. Indeed, he succeeded so well in being heard that he was publicly chastised—indeed, impeached—for making those speeches. Lincoln was cheered for keeping silent; Johnson was castigated for speaking to crowds. In our time, Dwight Eisenhower was criticized for not speaking out on a number of important policies, while Ronald Reagan has been hailed as the "great communicator" for his frequent popular appeals. To comprehend this sort of change—indeed, to identify it as change—one must be prepared to treat the political or-

16

der as an arena in which ideas matter. One must be prepared to reverse the common assumption that ideas are "epiphenomenal," that is, mere reflections of important political developments, and to entertain the possibility that thought might constitute politics.[21]

The Two Constitutional Presidencies

In the chapters to follow, I examine three expressions of constitutive thought in American politics: 1) *direct* expression of politically authoritative theories of the constitutional system and the presidency's place within it; 2) systemic understandings *indirectly* expressed through the array of rhetorical and political practices that amplify and express successive constitutional theories; and 3) ideas that emerge from the *conjunction* of systemic understandings, as modern presidents attempt to lead a nation under the auspices of two general, and conflicting, theories of the constitutional order.

American politics today, and American political development since the founding, can usefully be treated as a layered text. The first layer of this text-polity is formed by the political theory of the founders. Because subsequent attacks on that theory have sometimes gained public legitimacy without also altering constitutional and structural features of the regime, this thought can be viewed as superimposed upon the founding theory, altering without obliterating the original layer. The dilemmas of modern governance may be located, I argue, in that theoretical space between the layers of politically significant thought that form our political culture.

The modern presidency is buffeted by two "constitutions." Presidential action continues to be constrained and presidential behavior

---

[21] It is of course true that ideas can be no more than semi-independent variables in political development and that their relation to socio-economic circumstance, technology, and the like is in some sense reciprocal. It is worth noting, however, that students of politics feel less burden to add this sort of qualifying remark if they treat ideas as "epiphenomenal." The assumption that ideas have constitutive potential is a possibility to be entertained. It does not preclude the discovery that one is wrong, but the common assumption that ideas don't matter, once adopted, does not admit of a test of itself.

shaped by the original Constitution. The core structures established in 1789 and debated during the founding era remain essentially unchanged. For the most part, later amendments to the Constitution have left intact the basic features of the executive, legislative, and judicial branches of government. Great questions, such as the merits of unity or plurality in the executive, have not been seriously reopened. Because most of the structure persists, it is plausible that the theory upon which the presidency was constructed remains relevant to its current functioning.

At the same time, contemporary presidential and public understanding of the character of the constitutional system and of the president's place in it have changed. This new understanding is the "second constitution" under whose auspices presidents attempt to govern. Central to this second constitution is a view of statecraft that is in tension with the original Constitution—indeed, is opposed to the founder's understanding of the political system. The second constitution, which puts a premium on active and continuous presidential leadership of popular opinion, is buttressed by several extra-Constitutional factors such as the mass media and the proliferation of primaries as a mode of presidential selection.

Presidents work in a political system composed of elements in tension and, at times, in contradiction to one another. Presidents are taught to act as they do by the theory of leadership built into the constitutional structure, and reflected in its institutional principles and incentives. Simultaneously, a very different theory, which reflects current elite and public understanding of leadership, instructs, rewards, and punishes our chief executives. A central claim of this book is that the understanding of this ambivalent constitutional station is necessary to account for many of the dilemmas that attend modern presidential governance.

Chapter 2 is an analysis of the founding theory. To uncover that theory, I rely heavily upon *The Federalist*, a set of papers justifying the Constitution, written by three of its most articulate proponents, Alexander Hamilton, James Madison, and John Jay. The purpose of this journey back to the founders is not to point to their authority nor to lament change. Nor is it meant to imply that all of the supporters of the Constitution agreed with each of these arguments. *The Federalist* does represent, however, the most coherent systemic articulation of the implications of, and interconnections among, the principles and practices that were generally agreed upon when the Constitution was ratified. I then show how that theory is manifest and made more elaborate in formal modes of rhetoric established in the nineteenth century.

Informal political appeals in the nineteenth century are described in Chapter 3, to show the formative influence of the ruling doctrine upon political behavior. I discuss the character of informal speeches, the functions they were intended to serve, and the way they amplify the underlying constitutional perspective. A number of attempts by presidents to adopt practices now familiar to us were politically punished, further confirming the power of the original doctrine. Andrew Johnson's popular appeal is the most striking case of a campaign over the heads of Congress for legislation. The chapter concludes with a discussion of rhetoric's role in Johnson's impeachment.

Chapter 4 is an examination of the most successful use of popular leadership in American political history—Theodore Roosevelt's campaign to secure passage for a railroad regulation bill called the Hepburn Act. As the first president to secure legislation with an appeal "over the heads" of Congress to secure legislation, Roosevelt can lay some claim to being the father of the rhetorical presidency. His was a remarkable political achievement. The president's own party was against the bill. Few contemporary politicians believed he could win. Yet he won, and won big (346 to 7 in the House; 71 to 3 in the Senate).

I discuss this case for three reasons. First, it constitutes the first serious critique of the founding theory, which had proscribed popular leadership. Roosevelt did not speak solely of railroad regulation, but also spent considerable effort justifying his speaking in this way. The core of his argument was that a change in authorized practices was necessary to fulfill the purposes of the underlying founding theory of governance. So Roosevelt criticized the founding theory from within, displaying some of the dilemmas of governance built into the original arrangements.

Second, the case serves to highlight the exceptional conditions necessary, even today, for successful popular leadership. It serves as a paradigm of rhetorical leadership properly conceived and exercised. Franklin Roosevelt's campaign to pass the Social Security Act and Reagan's achievement of tax reform are two of a very few similar successes in American political history. I discuss the character of the special conditions conducive to that kind of success.

Finally, the case helps to explain how Woodrow Wilson's subsequent rejection of the constitutional perspective of the founders took hold when it did. By showing that the founders had not envisioned the full range of possibilities that their doctrine implied, Theodore Roosevelt prepared the country for the more radical critique that was to come in the administration of Woodrow Wilson.

Chapter 5 presents the theory of the "second constitution," the dominant understanding today that has been superimposed upon our original Constitution. To probe this theory I explore the political thought of Woodrow Wilson. Wilson self-consciously attacked *The Federalist* in his writings, since he regarded that book, as I do, as the best articulation of the meaning of the original Constitution. As president, Wilson tried to act according to the dictates of his reinterpretation of American politics. As I show through analysis of twentieth-century presidential rhetoric, presidents have continued to follow his example. Presidential scholars tend to echo his arguments. Of course, most presidents have not thought through the issues Wilson discussed—they are too busy for that. But if pushed and questioned, modern presidents would (and occasionally do) justify their behavior with arguments that echo Wilson's. Just as *The Federalist* represents the deepest and most coherent articulation of generally held nineteenth-century understandings, Wilson offers the most comprehensive theory in support of contemporary impulses and practices.[22]

---

[22] I should make clear that I am not claiming that modern presidents are self-conscious students of Wilson's writings. Just as college students often express, say, Freudian, Kantian, or Marxist arguments without ever having read the source, or

In this chapter I also compare the character and functions of rhetorical appeals in the nineteenth and twentieth centuries. I show a dramatic shift in the number of messages, the kinds of addresses that are offered, and the kinds of arguments that are contained in presidential messages in an effort to show the extent to which the second constitution dominates twentieth-century presidents' understandings of leadership.

After exploring the origins and development of the rhetorical presidency, I turn to the political significance and consequences of this political transformation. In Chapter 6, two cases detail the limits of modern leadership. The first case explores Woodrow Wilson's League of Nations fight and shows how that political battle and Wilson's rhetoric were structured by competing imperatives of the two constitutions. Wilson's political relation to the Senate, and his speech to them, was shaped by the old Constitution and reflected the theory it contains. His campaign to the people, and the character and content of his speeches, reflected his own new theory of his role, in tension with the old. His failure was not the defect of rhetorical ineptitude or, as many argue, of his personality. In spite of his skill, indeed his gift, Wilson was thwarted by the system he so successfully reinterpreted but only partially reconstituted.

The second case, Lyndon Johnson's War on Poverty effort, illustrates how apparent short-term rhetorical success (from an institutionally partisan perspective) resulted in long-term costs for the system as a whole. Johnson's preemption of the deliberative process resulted in a bill that even his supporters later conceded was poorly crafted, raised expectations without providing the means to reach them, and engendered other unforeseen consequences that might have been identified if the deliberative process had run its normal course. The case recalls Roosevelt's great individual ability to com-

---

even having known the name of the great thinker, so may contemporary presidents' views "echo" Wilson's without their being aware of it. Just as Freud is (almost always) more profound than the Freudian student who does not know Freud's name, so is Wilson more interesting than subsequent presidents who adopt his politics for reasons that they only dimly know.

bine a rhetorical campaign with traditional political skills. But Johnson's immediate legislative success brought with it long-term failure.

The cases of presidential failure are intended to reveal the limits of the rhetorical presidency and to illuminate some more general dilemmas of modern American politics. These dilemmas are the subject of Chapter 7. A fundamental dilemma is to provide institutional means for crises without making those crisis tools—and crises themselves—routine. The danger from the routinization of crisis is that the political system loses its ability to govern well between emergencies. The point cannot be stressed enough, however, that the executive energy needed to contend with crisis is a genuine need for which the original Constitution may have inadequately provided. Hence the dilemma.

Similarly, I explore the tradeoffs between synoptic change on the one hand and deliberation on the other. This problem is closely related to the tradeoff between increasing the president's power to make law and the costs of mutable law. These dilemmas are abstracted from the three preceding case studies, but are also illustrated by brief discussion of Ronald Reagan's rhetorical leadership, particularly his campaigns for tax reform, the budget of 1981, and the Strategic Defense Initiative.

Although I treat the founders' views more sympathetically than do most contemporary accounts of the presidency, I do not urge a simple return to the ways of the nineteenth century. Like a transparent overlay on an old map, the Wilsonian doctrine has altered the shape of the modern presidency without obliterating the original structure. Just as it is usually impossible for nations to restore ancient boundaries, it would now be difficult to reinstitute the founding perspective. Even if possible, it would not be desirable, because the Wilsonian critique, for all its problems, reveals flaws in our original Constitution.

My object is to describe and assess several fundamental problems of governance in modern America. I do not conclude with the customary wish list of political reforms. I am concerned less with prescribing new laws and practices than with contributing to the establishment of a condition in which intelligent public deliberation about reform would be possible. Hopefully, this book will aid that possibility by offering new terms with which to assess the character and development of the constitutional order and the president's place within it.

· 2 ·

THE OLD WAY:
FOUNDING AND FORMS

When Abraham Lincoln repeatedly refused to talk "policy" to assembled groups of citizens on his way from Illinois to Washington, D.C.; when Rutherford B. Hayes reported in his diary that he had reflected upon the propriety of sending a special message to Congress; when George Washington consulted his advisers as to the most appropriate form for his inaugural addresses—these presidents, like almost all others in the nineteenth century, were appealing to a common stock of political opinion and a family of rhetorical practices that constituted a doctrine. This chapter traces the origins and rationale for that doctrine, and illustrates its characteristic features expressed in formal modes of rhetoric. Chapter Three examines informal rhetoric and behavior, and assesses the extent to which the doctrine changed or developed throughout the nineteenth century.[1]

[1] Abraham Lincoln, "Speech at Pittsburgh, Pa., February 15, 1861," in *The Collected Works of Abraham Lincoln*, ed. Roy P. Basler, 9 vols. (New Brunswick, N.J.: Rutgers University Press, 1953–55), 4:210; Rutherford B. Hayes, *Diary and Letters of Rutherford B. Hayes*, ed. Charles Richard Williams, 6 vols. (Columbus: Ohio State Archeological and Historical Society, 1924), 3:447; James Thomas Flexner, *George Washington*, 4 vols. (Boston: Little, Brown & Co., 1969), 3: ch. 15; Douglas Southall Freeman, *George Washington*, 6 vols. (New York: Charles Scribner's Sons, 1954), 6:188.

Metaphorically, the doctrine can be considered a "common law" of rhetoric, since this set of prescriptions and proscriptions of modes of speech derived from constitutional principle but developed through various practices. Scholars in our time have not been very interested in the connections between these principles and practices. When these phenomena are mentioned, the focus is on the practices shorn of the opinions surrounding them. Replacing the opinions of founders and presidents is often the "theory" of the historian or political scientist, who suggests that these presidents generally opposed involvement in legislation or an energetic role in public policymaking and hence had no need for popular rhetoric. The nineteenth-century presidencies are viewed as valuable examples of the absence of twentieth-century practices, interesting for what they lack rather than for alternatives that they offer.

Yet the nineteenth-century doctrine was in fact robust, forward-looking, almost "up-to-date" in its conceptions of national politics. The nationalization of American politics, "big government," and a powerful presidency were all generated by the nineteenth-century constitutional order, prescribed by its most coherent partisans, and predicted by astute opponents of the constitutional polity.[2] The architects of the constitutional order and most nineteenth-century presidents believed that a strong national government led by a strong ex-

[2] While I rely upon the writings of Federalists, it is important to point out that many leading critics of the Constitution during the ratification campaign argued against the new government because of its national, strong executive properties. In their powerfully argued reservations to the proposed polity, which spoke of the virtues of legislative power, of decentralization, and of small government, the Anti-Federalists confirm the proposition that the Constitution can best be interpreted as facilitating the nationalization of American politics and the increase of executive power. See, for example, the essays of "Brutus," in *The Complete Anti-Federalist*, ed. Herbert J. Storing, 7 vols. (Chicago: University of Chicago Press, 1981), 2.9; and Herbert Storing's important study, *What the Anti-Federalists Were For* (Chicago: University of Chicago Press, 1981). The case for "big government" from the Federalist perspective is made by Storing as well: "The Problem of Big Government," in *A Nation of States*, ed. Robert Goldwin (New York: Rand McNally, 1963). For a contrary view, see Theodore Lowi, *The Personal President* (Ithaca, N.Y.: Cornell University Press, 1985), ch. 2.

ecutive was compatible with, indeed *required*, the proscription of most of the rhetorical practices that have now come to signify leadership.

CONSTITUTIONAL PRINCIPLES

To understand the place and character of presidential rhetoric in nineteenth-century American politics, we need to briefly outline four basic theoretical concerns that shaped the founders' understanding of the entire system. These are the issues of demagoguery, republicanism, independence of the executive, and separation of powers. The founders had other theoretical concerns, such as the issue of federalism, but these four were the core issues behind the practical structural decisions for the national government and the place of the presidency within it. One indication of their centrality is Woodrow Wilson's powerful attack on nineteenth-century practice (the subject of Chapter 5 below). Wilson explicitly based his reinterpretation of American politics upon a critique of these core constitutional considerations.

Demagoguery

The founders worried especially about the danger that a powerful executive might pose to the system if power were derived from the role of popular leader.[3] For most federalists, "demagogue" and "popular leader" were synonyms, and nearly all references to popular leaders in their writings are pejorative. Demagoguery, combined with

[3] *The Federalist* literally begins and ends with this issue. In the first number, "Publius" warns "that of those men who have overturned the liberties of republics, the greatest number have begun their career by paying obsequious court to the people, commencing demagogues and ending tyrants." And in the last essay, "These judicious reflections contain a lesson of moderation to all the sincere lovers of the Union, and ought to put them upon their guard against hazarding anarchy, civil war, and perhaps the military despotism of a victorious demagogue, in the pursuit of what they are not likely to obtain, but from TIME and EXPERIENCE."

majority tyranny, was regarded as the peculiar vice to which democracies were susceptible. While much historical evidence supported
this insight, the founders were made more acutely aware of the problem by the presence in their own midst of popular leaders such as
Daniel Shays, who led an insurrection in Massachusetts. The
founders' preoccupation with demagoguery may appear today as
quaint, yet it may be that we do not fear demagoguery today because
the founders were so successful in institutionally proscribing some
forms of it.

The original Greek meaning of ''demagogue'' was simply ''leader
of the people'' and the word was applied in premodern times to
champions of the people's claim to rule, as opposed to the claims of
aristocrats and monarchs. As James Ceaser points out, the term has
been more characteristically applied to a certain quality of leadership—that which attempts to sway popular passions. Since most
speech contains a mix of rational and passionate appeals, it is difficult to specify demagoguery with precision. But as Ceaser argues,
we cannot ignore the phenomenon simply because it is difficult to define, and he suggests that it possesses at least enough intuitive clarity
that few would label Dwight Eisenhower, for example, a demagogue, while most would not hesitate to so label Joseph McCarthy.
The key characteristic of demagoguery seems to be an excess of passionate appeals. Ceaser categorizes demagogues according to the
kinds of passions that are summoned, dividing these into ''soft'' and
''hard'' types.

The soft demagogue tends to flatter his constituents, ''by claiming
that they know what is best, and makes a point of claiming his closeness [to them] by manner or gesture.''[4] Hamilton focuses on this danger in the midst of a lengthy discussion of the need for sufficient du-

---

[4] James W. Ceaser, *Presidential Selection: Theory and Development* Princeton,
N.J.: Princeton University Press, 1979), 12, 54–60, 166–67, 318–27. See also
V. O. Key, *The Responsible Electorate* (New York: Random House, 1966), ch. 2;
Stanley Kelley Jr., *Political Campaigning: Problems in Creating an Informed Elec-
torate* (Washington, D.C.: Brookings Institution, 1960), 93; Pendleton E. Herring,
Presidential Leadership (New York: Rhinehart, 1940), 70.

ration of presidential tenure to protect the executive from servile pliancy to popular passion and to protect the people from a manipulative demagogue.

> It is a just observation that the people commonly *intend* the PUBLIC GOOD. This often applies to their very errors. But their good sense would despise the adulator who should pretend that they always *reason right* about the *means* of promoting it. They know from experience that they sometimes err; and the wonder is that they so seldom err as they do, beset as they continually are by the wiles of parasites and sycophants, by the snares of the ambitious, the avaricious, the desperate, by the artifices of men who possess their confidence more than they deserve it, and of those who seek to possess rather than to deserve it.[5]

In *The American Democrat*, James Fenimore Cooper wrote that demagoguery is the "peculiar danger of a democracy," and flattery the mark of a demagogue. "The man who is constantly telling people that they are unerring in judgment, and that they have all power, is a demagogue." By 1838, the danger appeared solely in its "soft" guise since the regime had legitimated majority rule and popular sovereignty, enabling "the demagogue [to] always [put] the people before the constitution and the laws, in face of the obvious truth that the people have placed the constitution and the laws before themselves." At the founding the problem of demagoguery was larger because the political stakes were higher, raising the prospect of "hard" demagoguery.[6]

The hard demagogue attempts to create or encourage divisions among the people in order to build and maintain his constituency. Typically, this sort of appeal employs extremist rhetoric that ministers to fear. James Madison worried about the possibility of class appeals that would pit the poor against the wealthy. But the "hard" demagogue might appeal to a very different passion. "Excessive encouragement of morality and hope" might be employed to create a division between those alleged to be compassionate, moral, or pro-

---

[5] *Federalist*, no. 71, p. 432.

[6] James Fenimore Cooper, *The American Democrat* (Indianapolis, Ind.: Liberty Classics, 1931 reprint; orig. publ. 1838), 101–102, 112–13, 120–28.

gressive, and those thought insensitive, selfish, or backward. Hard demagogues are not restricted to the ''right'' or to the ''left.''[7]

Demagogues also can be classified by their object. Here the issue becomes more complicated. Demagoguery might be good if it were a means to a good end, such as preservation of a decent nation or successful prosecution of a just war. The difficulty is to ensure by institutional means that demagoguery would tend to be employed for good ends and not simply for the satisfaction of overweening ambitions of immoral leaders or potential tyrants. How can political structures be created that permit demagoguery when appeals to passion are needed, but proscribe it for normal politics?

The founders did not have a straightforward answer to this problem, perhaps because there is no unproblematic institutional solution. Yet they did address it indirectly in two ways: they attempted both to narrow the range of acceptable demagogic appeals through the architectonic act of ''founding'' itself, and to mitigate the effects of such appeals in the day-to-day conduct of governance through the particular institutions they created. They did not choose to make provisions for the institutional encouragement of demagoguery in time of crisis, refusing to adopt, for example, the Roman model of constitutional dictatorship for emergencies.[8]

Many references in *The Federalist* and in the ratification debates warn of demagogues of the hard variety who through divisive appeals would aim at tyranny. *The Federalist* literally begins and ends with this issue. In the final paper Hamilton offers ''a lesson of moderation to all sincere lovers of the Union [that] ought to put them on their guard against hazarding anarchy, civil war, a perpetual alienation of the states from each other, and perhaps the military despotism

---

[7] *Federalist*, no. 10, p. 82; Ceaser, *Presidential Selection*, 324.

[8] Clinton Rossiter, *Constitutional Dictatorship: Crisis Government in the Modern Democracies* (Princeton, N.J.: Princeton University Press, 1948), ch. 3. Behind their indirect approach may have been the thought that excessive ambition needs no institutional support and the faith that in extraordinary circumstances, popular rhetoric, even forceful demagoguery, would gain legitimacy through the pressure of necessity.

of a victorious demagogue. . . .'"[9] This concern with ''hard'' demagoguery at the founding was not merely, though it was partly, a rhetorical device itself designed to facilitate passage of the Constitution. It also reveals a concern to address the kinds of divisions and issues exploited by ''hard'' demagoguery. From this perspective, the founding can be understood as an attempt to settle the large issue of whether the one, the few, or the many would rule (in favor of the many ''through'' a constitution); to reconfirm the limited purposes of government (security, prosperity, and the protection of rights); and thereby to give effect to the distinction between public and private life. At the founding, these large questions were still matters of political dispute. Hamilton argued that adoption of the Constitution would settle these perennially divisive questions for Americans, replacing those questions with smaller, less contentious issues. Hamilton called this new American politics a politics of ''administration,'' distinguishing it from the traditional politics of disputed ends. If politics were transformed and narrowed in this way, thought Hamilton, demagogues would be deprived of part of their once-powerful arsenal of rhetorical weapons because certain topics would be rendered illegitimate for public discussion. By constituting an American understanding of politics, the founding would also reconstitute the problem of demagoguery.

I have briefly described some foundational tenets of modern liberalism. The founders were not the first liberals, of course. They reflected the mode of reasoning and form of argument of liberal political philosophy.[10] Like the liberal theorists, the founders seldom

[9] Harvey Flaumenhaft, ''Hamilton's Administrative Republic and the American Presidency,'' in *The Presidency in the Constitutional Order*, ed. Joseph M. Bessette and Jeffrey Tulis (Baton Rouge and London: Louisiana State University Press, 1981), 65–114. Of course, the Civil War, and turn-of-the-century progressive politics discussed in Chapter Three below, show that Hamilton's ''administrative republic'' has been punctuated with the sorts of crises and politics he sought to avoid.

[10] In speaking of the founders as ''liberals,'' I mean to include the Anti-Federalists along with the Federalists. As the Anti-Federalist ''Agrippa'' stated, ''Both parties . . . found[ed] their arguments on the idea that these [individual] rights ought to be held sacred.'' *Essays on the Constitution of the United States*, ed. Paul Leicester

wrote about rhetoric directly. This poses a small research problem; how are we to discover their understanding of political rhetoric? The answer to the research problem turns out to be an insight into the character of liberal politics, for rhetoric is taught indirectly in liberal polities. Because liberal theorists and the founders were so concerned to circumscribe politics, to narrow the public sphere, they generally addressed problems of rhetoric indirectly, through discussions of institutions.

Moreover, as I shall argue, the principal actors in the government would be taught rhetorical practice through institutional mores, incentives, and rewards. To see how it could be otherwise, consider the fact that Aristotle, Quintilian, and Cicero, all of whom lived in polities whose governments penetrated deeply into what we consider the private sphere, wrote treatises on rhetoric and addressed them directly to rhetoricians. As Carnes Lord has shown, Aristotle, for example, attempted to persuade young rhetoricians to follow his precepts rather than their instincts or the precepts of sophists and well-known contemporaries, in order to control tendencies toward demagoguery.[11] There are no comparable treatises on rhetoric by the political philosophers most consulted by the founders (Locke, Hume, Montesquieu, etc.).[12] Replacing a doctrine of rhetoric or theory of

Ford (Brooklyn, N.Y.: Historical Printing Club, 1892), 61–62. A probing study that makes the connection of liberalism and leadership its theme is Robert Eden, *Political Leadership and Nihilism* (Gainesville: University of Florida Press, 1984).

[11] Carnes Lord, "Aristotle's Poetics and Rhetoric" (Ph.D. dissertation, Cornell University, 1970). For a contrary thesis on Aristotle's intention, see Larry Arnhart, "Aristotle on Political Reasoning: A Commentary on the *Rhetoric* (Ph.D. dissertation, University of Chicago, 1977).

[12] Hume did discuss certain problems of modern style in "Of Eloquence," a short discourse in his *Essays*, but he did not write a treatise or substantial theory. A possible exception is Hobbes, from whom we have two treatises on rhetoric and one on sophistry. Most of this material is an abridgment of Aristotle's *Rhetoric*, however. Like Marx, who was to translate Aristotle's *Rhetoric* later, Hobbes appears uninterested in instructing rhetoricians, but rather intrigued by the political understanding of the work, and by the analysis of the passions in particular. Thomas Hobbes, "The Whole Art of Rhetoric," "The Art of Rhetoric," and "The Art of Sophistry," in *The English Works of Thomas Hobbes*, ed. Sir William Molesworth, 10 vols. (London, 1839), 6:423 ff, 511 ff. Karl Marx, "Letter to His Father: On a Turning Point

persuasion addressed directly to political actors are sets of teachings on the building of institutions. It is primarily in discussions of the principles underlying the major national institutions that the founders addressed the problems of rhetoric. And it is through analysis of these institutional structures and practices that we can reconstitute an American rhetorical doctrine.

If the overriding concern about demagoguery in the extraordinary period before ratification of the Constitution was to prevent social disruption, division, and possibly tyranny, the concerns expressed through the Constitution for normal times were broader: to create institutions that would be most likely to generate and execute good policy or be most likely to resist bad policy. Underlying the institutional structures and powers created by the Constitution are three principles designed to address this broad concern: representation, independence of the executive, and separation of powers.

Representation

As the founders realized, the problem with any simple distinction between good and bad law is that it is difficult to provide clear criteria to distinguish the two in any particular instance. It will not do to suggest that in a democracy good legislation reflects the majority will. A majority may tyrannize a minority, violating its rights; even a non-tyrannical majority may be a foolish one, preferring policies that do not further its interests. Finally, the factual quest to find a "majority" may be no less contestable than a dispute over the merits of proposals. Contemporary political scientists provide ample support for the latter worry when they suggest that it is often both theoretically and practically impossible to discover a majority will—that is, to count it up—due to the manifold differences of intensity of preferences and the plethora of possible hierarchies of preferences. These

---

in His Life (1837)," in *Writings of Young Marx on Philosophy and Society*, ed. Lloyd D. Easton and Kurt H. Guddet (New York: Doubleday & Co., 1967), 47.

considerations lie behind the distrust of ''direct'' or ''pure'' democracy.[13]

Yet an alternative understanding—that legislation is good if it objectively furthers the limited ends of the polity—is also problematic. It is perhaps impossible to assess the interests of a nation without giving considerable attention to what the citizenry considers its interests to be. This consideration lies behind the animus toward monarchy and aristocracy.[14] Identifying and embodying the proper weight to give popular opinion and the appropriate institutional reflections of it is one of the characteristic problems of democratic constitutionalism. The founders' understanding of republicanism as representative government reveals this problem and the Constitution's attempted solution.

Practically, the founders attempted to accommodate these two requisites of good government by four devices. First, they established popular election as the fundamental basis of the Constitution and of the government's legitimacy. They modified that requirement by allowing ''indirect'' selection for some institutions (e.g., the Senate, Supreme Court, presidency)—that is, selection by others who were themselves chosen by the people. With respect to the president, the founders wanted to elicit the ''sense of the people,'' but they feared an inability to do so if the people acted in a ''collective capacity.'' They worried that the dynamics of mass politics would at best produce poorly qualified presidents and at worst open the door to demagoguery and regime instability. At the same time, the founders wanted to give popular opinion a greater role in presidential selection than it would have if Congress chose the executive. The institutional solution to these concerns was the Electoral College, originally de-

[13] *Federalist*, no. 10, p. 77; no. 43, p. 276; no. 51, pp. 323–25; no. 63, p. 384; no. 73, p. 443. Kenneth Arrow, *Social Choice and Individual Values* (New York: John Wiley & Sons, 1963); Benjamin I. Page, *Choices and Echoes in Presidential Elections* (Chicago: University of Chicago Press, 1978), ch. 2.

[14] *Federalist*, no. 39, p. 241; see also Martin Diamond, ''Democracy and the Federalist: A Reconsideration of the Framers' Intent,'' *American Political Science Review* 53 (March 1959): 52–68.

signed as a semi-autonomous locus of decision for presidential selection, and chosen by state legislatures at each election.[15]

Second, the founders established differing lengths of tenure for officeholders in the major national institutions, which corresponded to the institutions' varying proximities to the people. House members were to face reelection every two years, thus making them more responsive to constituent pressure than members of the other national institutions. The president was given a four-year term, sufficient time, it was thought, to "contribute to the firmness of the executive" without justifying "any alarm for the public liberty."[16]

Third, the founders derived the authority and formal power of the institutions and their officers ultimately from the people but immediately from the Constitution, thus insulating officials from day-to-day currents of public opinion, while leaving scope for assertion of deeply felt and widely shared public opinion through constitutional amendment.

Finally, the founders envisioned that the extent of the nation itself would insulate governing officials from sudden shifts of public opinion. In his well-known arguments for an extended republic, Madison reasoned that large size would improve democracy by making the formation of majority factions difficult. But again, argued Madison, extent of the territory and diversity of factions would not prevent the formation of a majority if the issue were an important one.[17]

It is the brakes upon public opinion rather than the provision for its

[15] *Federalist*, no. 39, p. 241; no. 68, pp. 412–23. See also James Ceaser, "Presidential Selection," in *The Presidency in the Constitutional Order*, ed. Bessette and Tulis, 234–82. Ironically, the founders were proudest of this institutional creation; the Electoral College was their most original contrivance. Moreover, it escaped the censure of and even won a good deal of praise from anti-federalist opponents of the Constitution. Because electors were chosen by state legislatures for the sole purpose of selecting a president, the process was thought *more* democratic than potential alternatives, such as selection by Congress.

[16] *Federalist*, no. 71, p. 435. The empirical judgment that four years would serve the purpose of insulating the president is not as important for this discussion as the principle reflected in that choice, a principle that has fueled recent calls for a six-year term.

[17] *Federalist*, no. 9; no. 10.

35

influence that causes skepticism today.[18] Because popular leadership is so central to modern theories of the presidency, the rationale behind the founders' distrust of "direct democracy" should be noted specifically. This issue is joined dramatically in *The Federalist*, no. 49, in which Madison addresses Jefferson's suggestion that "whenever two of the three branches of government shall concur in [the] opinion . . . that a convention is necessary for altering the Constitution, *or correcting breaches of it*, a convention shall be called for the purpose." Madison recounts Jefferson's reasoning: because the Constitution was formed by the people, it rightfully ought to be modified by them. Madison admits "that a constitutional road to the decision of the people ought to be marked out and kept open, for certain great and extraordinary occasions." But he objects to bringing directly to the people disputes among the branches about the extent of their authority. In the normal course of governance, such disputes could be expected to arise fairly often. In our day they would include, for example, the war powers controversy, the impoundment controversy, and the issue of executive privilege.

Madison objects to recourse to "the people" on three basic grounds. First, popular appeals would imply "some defect" in the government: "Frequent appeals would, in great measure, deprive the government of that veneration which time bestows on everything, and without which perhaps the wisest and freest governments would not possess the requisite stability." *The Federalist* points to the institutional benefits of popular veneration—stability of government and the enhanced authority of its constitutional officers. Second, the tranquility of the society as a whole might be disturbed. Madison expresses the fear that an enterprising demagogue might reopen disputes over "great national questions" in a political context less favorable to their resolution than the constitutional convention.

---

[18] Gordon Wood, *The Creation of the American Republic 1776–1787* (New York: W. W. Norton, 1969); Michael Parenti, "The Constitution As an Elitist Document," in *How Democratic Is the Constitution?* ed. Robert Goldwin (Washington, D.C.: American Enterprise Institute, 1980), 39–58; Charles Lindblom, *Politics and Markets* (New York: Basic Books, 1979), Conclusion.

Finally, Madison voices "the greatest objection of all" to frequent appeals to the people: "the decisions which would probably result from such appeals would not answer the purpose of maintaining the constitutional equilibrium of the government." The executive might face political difficulties if frequent appeals to the people were permitted because other features of his office (his singularity, independence, and executive powers) would leave him at a rhetorical disadvantage in contests with the legislature. Presidents would be "generally the objects of jealousy and their administration[s] . . . liable to be discolored and rendered unpopular," Madison argues. "[T]he members of the legislative department on the other hand are numerous. . . . Their connections of blood, of friendship, and of acquaintance embrace a great proportion of the most influential part of the society. The nature of their public trust implies a personal influence among the people. . . ."[19]

Madison realizes that there may be circumstances "less adverse to the executive and judiciary departments." If the executive power were "in the hands of a peculiar favorite of the people . . . the public decision might be less swayed by prepossessions in favor of the legislative party. But still it could never be expected to turn on the true merits of the question." The ultimate reason for the rejection of "frequent popular appeals" is that they would undermine deliberation and result in bad public policy:

> The *passions*, therefore, not the *reason*, of the public would sit in judgment. But it is the reason, alone, of the public, that ought to control and regulate the government. The passions ought to be controlled and regulated by the government.[20]

There are two frequent misunderstandings about the founders' opinion on the "deliberative" function of representation. The first is that they naively believed that deliberation constituted the whole of legislative politics—that there would be no bargaining, logrolling, or nondeliberative rhetorical appeals. The discussion of Congress in

[19] *Federalist*, no. 49, pp. 313–17.
[20] Ibid., 317.

The Federalist, nos. 52 to 68, and in the constitutional convention debates, reveals quite clearly that the founders understood that the legislative process would involve a mixture of these elements. The founding task was to create an institutional context that made deliberation more likely, not to assume that it would occur naturally or, even in the best of legislatures, predominantly.[21]

The second common error, prevalent in leading historical accounts of the period, is to interpret the deliberative elements of the founders' design as an attempt to rid the legislative councils of "common men" and replace them with "better sorts"—more educated and above all more propertied individuals.[22] Deliberation, in this view, is the byproduct of the kind of person elected to office. The public's opinions are "refined and enlarged" because refined individuals do the governing. Although this view finds some support in *The Federalist* and was a worry of several Anti-Federalists, the founders' Constitution places much greater emphasis upon the formal structures of the national institutions than upon the backgrounds of officeholders.[23] Indeed, good character and high intelligence, they reasoned, would be of little help to the government if it resembled a direct democracy: "In all very numerous assemblies, of whatever characters composed, passion never fails to wrest the sceptre from reason. Had every Athenian citizen been a Socrates, every Athenian assembly would still have been a mob."[24] As we shall see, some of the modes

[21] See *Federalist*, no. 57; Joseph M. Bessette, "Deliberative Democracy," in *How Democratic Is the Constitution?* ed. Robert Goldwin, 102–116; Michael Malbin, "What Did the Founders Want Congress To Be—and Who Cares?" paper presented to the American Political Science Association, Denver, Colo., September 2, 1982. On the status of legislative deliberation today, see Joseph M. Bessette, *Deliberation in Congress* (Ph.D. dissertation, University of Chicago, 1977); William Muir, *Legislature* (Chicago: University of Chicago Press, 1982); and Arthur Maas, *Congress and the Common Good* (New York: Basic Books, 1983).

[22] Wood, *Creation of the American Republic*, ch. 5; Ceaser, *Presidential Selection*, 48.

[23] *Federalist*, no. 62 and no. 63, pp. 376–90; "Agrippa," in *The Antifederalists*, ed. Cecilia M. Kenyon (New York: Bobbs Merrill Co., 1966), 134–60.

[24] *Federalist*, no. 55, p. 342; Max Farrand, ed., *The Records of the Federal Convention of 1787*, 4 vols. (New Haven, Conn.: Yale University Press, 1966), 1:53.

of rhetoric emerged as part of the formal structure designed to encourage deliberation.

The presidency thus was intended to be representative of the people, but not merely responsive to popular will. Drawn from the people through an election (albeit an indirect one), the president was to be free enough from the daily shifts in public opinion so that he could refine it and, paradoxically, better serve popular interests. Hamilton expresses well this element of the theory in a passage in which he links the problem of representation to that of demagoguery:

> There are some who would be inclined to regard the servile pliancy of the executive to a prevailing current, either in the community or in the legislature, as its best recommendation. But such men entertain very crude notions, as well of the purposes for which government was instituted, as of the true means by which the public happiness may be promoted. The republican principle demands that the deliberative sense of the community should govern the conduct of those to whom they intrust the management of their affairs; but it does not require an unqualified complaisance to every sudden breeze of passion, or to every transient impulse which the people may receive from the arts of men, who flatter their prejudices to betray their interests. . . . [W]hen occasions present themselves in which the interests of the people are at variance with their inclinations, it is the duty of the persons whom they have appointed to be the guardians of those interests to withstand the temporary delusion in order to give them time and opportunity for more cool and sedate reflection. . . .[25]

Independence of the Executive

In order to "withstand the temporary delusions" of popular opinion, the executive was made independent. The office would draw its

[25] *Federalist*, no. 71, p. 432; Madison expresses almost the identical position in no. 63, where he states, "As the cool and deliberate sense of the community, ought, in all governments, and actually will, in all free governments, ultimately prevail over the views of its rulers; so there are particular moments in public affairs when the people, stimulated by some irregular passion, or some illicit advantage, or misled by the artful misrepresentations of interested men, may call for measures which they themselves will afterwards be most ready to lament and condemn. In these critical moments how salutary will be . . . [a Senate]."

authority from the Constitution rather than from another governmental branch. The framers were led to this decision from their knowledge of the states, where, according to John Marshall, the governments (with the exception of New York) lacked any structure that ''could resist the wild projects of the moment, give the people an opportunity to reflect and allow the good sense of the nation time for exertion.'' As Madison stated at the convention, ''Experience had proved a tendency in our governments to throw all power into the legislative vortex. The executives of the states are in general little more than Cyphers; the legislatures omnipotent. . . .''[26]

While independence from Congress was the immediate practical need, it was a need based upon the close connection between legislatures and popular opinion. Because independence from public opinion was the source of concern about the legislatures, the founders rejected James Wilson's arguments on behalf of popular election as a means of making the president independent of Congress.

The independence of the executive created the conditions under which presidents would be most likely to adopt a different perspective from Congress on matters of public policy. Congress would be dominated by local factions that, according to plan, would give great weight to constituent opinion. The president, as Thomas Jefferson was to argue, was the only national officer ''who commanded a view of the whole ground.'' Metaphorically, independence gave the president his own ''space'' within, and his own angle of vision upon, the polity. According to the founding theory, these constituent features of discretion are entailed by the twin activities of executing the will of the legislature *and* leading a legislature to construct good laws to be executed, laws that would be responsive to long-term needs of the nation at large.[27]

---

[26] John Marshall, *Life of George Washington*, quoted in Charles Thatch, *The Creation of the Presidency*, reprint (Baltimore: Johns Hopkins University Press, 1969), 51; Farrand, *Records*, 2:35; 2:22, 32.

[27] *Federalist*, no. 68, p. 413; no. 71, p. 433; no. 73, p. 442; see also Storing, ''Introduction,'' in Thatch, *Creation of the Presidency*, pp. vi–viii; Thomas Jefferson, Inaugural Address, March 4, 1801.

Separation of Powers

The constitutional role of the president in lawmaking raises the question of the meaning and purpose of separation of powers. What is the sense of "separation of power" if power is shared among the branches of government? In the 1940s and 1950s, political scientists easily refuted those legalists who assumed that the founders wanted to distinguish so carefully among executive, legislative, and judicial power as to make each the exclusive preserve of a particular branch. However, the legalistic error has given rise to another.

Political scientists, following Richard Neustadt, have assumed that since powers were not divided according to the principle of "one branch, one function," the founders made no principled distinction among kinds of power. Instead, according to Neustadt, they created "separate institutions sharing power."[28] The premise of that claim is that power is an entity that can be divided up to prevent any one branch from having enough to rule another. In this view, the sole purpose of separation of powers is to preserve liberty by preventing the arbitrary rule of any one center of power.

The Neustadt perspective finds some support in the founders' deliberations, and in the Constitution. Much attention was given to making each branch "weighty" enough to resist encroachment by the others. Yet this "checks and balances" view of separation of powers can be understood better in tandem with an alternative understanding of the concept. Powers were separated and structures of each branch differentiated in order to equip each branch to perform different tasks. Each branch would be superior (although not the sole power) in its own sphere and in its own way. The purpose of separation of powers was to make effective governance more likely.[29]

[28] Richard Neustadt, *Presidential Power*, 3rd ed. (New York: John Wiley & Sons, 1980; orig. publ. 1960), 26, 28–30, 170, 176, 204. See also James Sterling Young, *The Washington Community* (New York: Columbia University Press, 1964), 53. This insight has been the basis of numerous critiques of the American "pluralist" system, which allegedly frustrates leadership as it forces politicians through a complicated political obstacle course.

[29] Farrand, *Records*, 1:66–67; *Federalist*, no. 47, pp. 360–80; see especially Storing, *What the Anti-Federalists Were For*, 60–61. See also U.S. Congress, *Annals*,

Ensuring the protection of liberty and individual rights was one element of effective governance as conceived by the founders, but not the only one. Government also needed to ensure the security of the nation and to implement policies that reflected popular will.[30] These three governmental objectives might conflict; for example, popular opinion might favor policies that violate rights. Separation of powers was thought to be an institutional way of accommodating the tensions between governmental objectives.

Table 2.1 presents a simplified view of the purposes behind the separation of powers. Note that the three objectives of government—popular will, popular rights, and self-preservation—are mixed twice in the Constitution: they are mixed among the branches and within each branch so that each objective is given priority in one branch. Congress and the president were to concern themselves with all three, but the priority of their concern differs, with "self-preservation" or national security of utmost concern to the president.

The term "separation of powers" perhaps has obstructed understanding of the extent to which different structures were designed to give each branch the special quality needed to secure its governmental objectives. Thus, while the founders were not so naive as to expect that Congress would be simply "deliberative," they hoped that its plural membership and bicameral structure would provide necessary, if not sufficient, conditions for deliberation to emerge. Similarly, the president's energy, it was hoped, would be enhanced by unity, the prospect of reelection, and substantial discretion. As we all know, the Court does not simply "judge" dispassionately; it also makes policies and exercises will. But the founders believed that it made no sense to have a Supreme Court if it were intended to be just

---

1:384–412, 476–608; Louis Fisher, *Constitutional Conflict between Congress and President* (Princeton, N.J.: Princeton University Press, 1985). Cf. M.J.C. Vile, *Constitutionalism and the Separation of Powers* (London: Oxford University Press, 1967), ch. 1.

[30] In many discussions of separation of powers today, the meaning of "effectiveness" is restricted to only one of these objectives—the implementation of policy that reflects popular will. See, for example, Donald Robinson, ed., *Reforming American Government* (Boulder, Colo.: Westview Press, 1985).

TABLE 2.1 Separation of Powers

Objectives (in order of priority)	Special Qualities and Functions (to be aimed at)	Structures and Means
CONGRESS		
1. popular will	deliberation	a. plurality
2. popular rights		b. proximity (frequent House elections)
3. self-preservation		c. bicameralism
		d. competent powers
PRESIDENT		
1. self-preservation	energy and "steady administration of law"	a. unity
2. popular rights		b. four-year term and eligibility
3. popular will		c. competent powers
COURT		
1. popular rights	"judgment, not will"	a. small collegial body
		b. life tenure
		c. power linked to argument

like a Congress. The judiciary was structured to make the dispassionate protection of rights more likely, if by no means certain.

The founders differentiated powers as well as structures in the original design. These powers ("the executive power," vested in the president in Article II, and "all legislative power herein granted," given to Congress in Article I) overlap and sometimes conflict. Yet both the legalists' view of power as "parchment distinction" and the political scientists' view of "separate institutions sharing power" provide inadequate guides to what happens and what was thought ought to happen when powers collided. The founders urged that "line-drawing" among spheres of authority be the product of political conflict among the branches, not the result of dispassionate legal analysis. While not dispassionate, this political conflict would be constrained and structured, in part, by parchment arguments, debate over the principles that informed the Constitution. Contrary to more contemporary views, they did not believe that such conflict would lead to deadlock or stalemate.[31]

Consider the disputes that sometimes arise from claims of "executive privilege."[32] Presidents occasionally refuse to provide Congress with information that its members deem necessary to carry out their special functions, usually justifying assertions of executive privilege on the grounds of either national security or the need to maintain the conditions necessary to sound execution, including the unfettered canvassing of options.

Both Congress and the president have legitimate constitutional prerogatives at stake: Congress has a right to know and the president has a need for secrecy. How does one discover whether in any particular instance the president's claim is more or less weighty than Congress's? The answer will depend upon the circumstances—for example, the importance of the particular piece of legislation in the congressional agenda versus the importance of the particular secret to the executive. There is no formula independent of political circumstance with which to weigh such competing institutional claims. The most knowledgeable observers of those political conflicts are the parties themselves: Congress and the president.

Each branch has weapons at its disposal to use against the other. Congress can threaten to hold up legislation or appointments important to the president. Ultimately, it could impeach him. For his part, a president may continue to "stonewall"; he may veto bills or fail to support legislation of interest to his legislative opponents; he may delay political appointments; and he may put the issue to a public test, even submitting to an impeachment inquiry for his own advantage. The lengths to which presidents and Congresses are willing to go was thought to be a rough measure of the importance of their respective constitutional claims. Nearly always, executive–legislative disputes

[31] See, for example, Lloyd Cutler, "To Form a Government," *Foreign Affairs* (Fall 1980): 126–43.

[32] Gary J. Schmitt, "Executive Privilege: Presidential Power to Withhold Information from Congress," in *The Presidency in the Constitutional Order*, ed. Bessette and Tulis, 154–94.

are resolved at a relatively low stage of potential conflict. In 1981, for example, President Reagan ordered Interior Secretary James Watt to release information to a Senate committee after the committee had agreed to maintain confidentiality. The compromise was reached after public debate and "contempt of Congress" hearings were held.

This political process is dynamic. Viewed at particular moments the system may appear deadlocked; considered over time, substantial movement becomes apparent. Similar scenarios could be constructed for the other issues over which congressional and presidential claims to authority conflict, such as the use of executive agreements in place of treaties, the deployment of military force, or the executive impoundment of appropriated monies.[33]

From the founding point of view, conflict between the branches should be encouraged by the system. To do so in ways that would produce beneficial results, the Constitution had to prescribe forms of political behavior consonant with the special tasks and perspectives of each governmental branch. For separation of powers to work, how legislators and presidents were to act was to be as important as what they would stand for. Indeed, from the point of view of institutional theorists like the founders, there was no greater political problem than to establish the ways in which politicians would be encouraged to behave—that is, the forms of political activity.

OFFICIAL RHETORIC

The founding understanding of the problems of demagoguery, representation, independence of the executive, and separation of powers resulted in a presidency that embodied the myriad demands of repub-

---

[33] Richard Pious, *The American Presidency* (New York: Basic Books, 1979), 372–415; Gary J. Schmitt, "Separation of Powers: Introduction to the Study of Executive Agreements," *American Journal of Jurisprudence*, vol. 27 (1982): 114–38; Louis Fisher, *Presidential Spending Power* (Princeton, N.J.: Princeton University Press, 1975), 147–201.

licanism in a new and peculiarly American way. Freed from the need
to consult the people continually, the president was nevertheless to
be judged by them periodically; independent enough to be forceful
and preeminent in matters of command, he remained an unequal
partner in the deliberative process; and situated in an office in which
demagoguery could be most harmful, he would be constrained by
structures and practices that made it unprofitable and unlikely. The
development of presidential rhetoric in the nineteenth century reflected the force of the general constitutional theory. Two general
prescriptions for presidential speech emerged.

First, policy rhetoric—that is, recommendations for new laws, or
detailed descriptions of the state of the union with suggestions for
change—would be *written*, and addressed principally to *Congress*.
Of course, some presidents could be expected to try to speak to the
people through these messages; but since these addresses would be
directed in the first instance to Congress, the rhetoric would be constrained by the written form and the character of the immediate audience. To the extent that the people read these speeches, they would
be called upon to raise their understanding to the level of deliberative
speech.

Embodying two demands of republicanism, rhetoric to Congress
would be *public* (available to all) but not thereby *popular* (fashioned
for all). The Constitution contains this principle in two of its provisions. In Article I, Section 7, attached to the presidential privilege of
a veto, is the president's duty to present Congress with a veto message, stating "his objections to that House in which the bill shall
have originated, who shall enter the objections at large on their journal, and proceed to reconsider it." And in Article II, Section 3, another deliberative duty is placed upon the president: "He shall from
time to time give to the Congress information on the State of the
Union, and recommend to their consideration such measures as he
shall judge necessary and expedient." The Constitution does not say
that such rhetoric shall be written, although the veto clause implies
it. But, following principles of the general theory of the Constitution,
early presidents and Congresses assumed that written messages were
constitutionally prescribed.

Second, rhetoric that was directed primarily to the people at large developed along lines consistent with the case against popular leadership. Nowhere are they mentioned in the Constitution, but the practices of issuing proclamations and offering an inaugural address were instituted in the first presidency with attention to their constitutional propriety. The inaugural address, for example, developed along lines that emphasized popular instruction in constitutional principle and the articulation of the general tenor and direction of presidential policy, while tending to avoid discussion of the merits of particular policy proposals.

Like many other institutions and practices, the specific forms of presidential rhetoric were not discussed, let alone settled, during the convention and ratification debate. Like the status of the executive departments, the specific modes of rhetoric were left for determination by early Congresses and presidents. George Washington was particularly sensitive to the need to establish constitutionally informed, useful precedents—so much so that he devoted considerable time during his first year as president to decisions regarding the symbolic dimension of his office. These included: when and in what manner to appear before Congress; when and how to receive congressmen at the White House; how to establish the protocol between the president and governors of the states; with whom the president should stay while on official excursion; and how his daily "line of conduct" and style of living should be managed so as to enhance the dignity of his office while supporting popular attachment to republicanism.[34] Most important for present purposes, Washington devoted considerable time to deciding upon the appropriate modes of rhetoric.

Inaugural Addresses

After extensive preparation, Washington offered the first of what would be three predominant types of inaugural address in the nineteenth century. The first president used the occasion to praise vir-

[34] James Hart, *The American Presidency in Action: 1789* (New York: Macmillan Co., 1948), ch. 2.

tuous men, to display his own character and virtue, and to implore fellow officers of the government to take their guidance from the Constitution and from "that Almighty Being who rules over the Universe." Washington refused to talk policy. Indeed, he had originally prepared a seventy-three-page set of recommendations to Congress as his first draft of the Inaugural, thinking that he would speak as part of his constitutional duty to "recommend measures to Congress." He discarded the draft, as he mentions in the final speech itself, because the circumstances seemed inappropriate.[35] Just what the circumstances required never became clear to Washington. He took his oath before "the people" assembled outdoors, but delivered his remarks to a select audience of congressmen and dignitaries and addressed the remarks to "Fellow Citizens of the Senate and House of Representatives," not to the people at large as all presidents after Adams were to do.

The first inaugural ceremony had some resemblance to a royal appearance before Parliament, and when Washington concluded his oath, the Chancellor (of New York, who administered the oath) proclaimed, "Long Live George Washington, President of the United States."[36] Washington was groping for a model of speech and ceremony that would establish the dignity of his office but not appear monarchical. His peculiar difficulty was to offer a republican but nonpopular address. Glen Thurow analyzed his solution as follows:

> He tries to make himself as good an example as possible for the assembled Congressmen and for those who are to follow. He displays his patriotism, his sense of duty, his loyalty to the Constitution, and his freedom from creed or vain ambition throughout the speech. Washington sees the powers and responsibilities of his office as stemming from the Constitution and hence, only indirectly from the people. It is only through the force of his example that he could be said to have a direct relationship to the people in the speech. His outstanding qualities provide a model for other politicians, and attracts the people at large to their government. This model helps to infuse the Constitution with the

[35] James T. Flexner, *George Washington and the New Nation, 1783–1793*, 6 vols. (Boston: Little, Brown & Co., 1969), 6:183; James Southall Freeman, *George Washington*, 6 vols. (New York: Charles Scribner's Sons, 1954), 6:188.
[36] Flexner, *George Washington*, 187.

proper spirit. But Washington's relationship to the people is not the grounds of either his powers or his duties.[37]

In its immediate hearing the speech was successful. The famous orator Fisher Ames "watched entranced and with some resentment" that such a simple display of character "so denied the importance of the elocutionist's art." "It seemed to me," he wrote, "an allegory in which virtue was personified, and addressing those whom she would make her votaries."[38] Biographer James Flexner reports that the entire audience, including the envious John Adams, was in tears.

Yet Washington did not regard the speech a success. While the Address eschewed policy rhetoric and made no place for demagoguery or the flourishes of high oratory, Washington worried that its emphasis on virtue and, more particularly, the pomp attendant to the ceremony might too easily and wrongly be imitated by future presidents aspiring to monarchy.[39] Therefore, four years later, at the time of his second inauguration, Washington remained virtually silent, offering only two short paragraphs (this time to all "Fellow Citizens"), in which he promises to speak later if the occasion is proper to thank the citizenry for "the confidence which has been reposed in me" (perhaps alluding to a Farewell Address), and he pledges not to violate the oath of office.[40]

John Adams attempted to revive the form of the first inaugural and produced the type of speech Washington feared. Thurow perceptively describes it as an unintentional parody of Washington's first Address that "led to a somewhat ludicrous defense of Adams' own patriotism and to a grudging acquiescence in the Congressional acclaim of Washington's greatness—all, incidently, in a sentence that must be the longest and most convoluted in the history of American political oratory."[41]

[37] Glen E. Thurow, "Voice of the People: Speechmaking and the Modern Presidency," address delivered at Wake Forest University, October 1, 1979, p. 9.

[38] Quoted in Flexner, *George Washington*, 188.

[39] Thurow, "Voice of the People," 10.

[40] *Inaugural Addresses of the Presidents of the United States* (Washington, D.C.: Government Printing Office, 1952), 4.

[41] Thurow, "Voice of the People," 12.

Jefferson reconstituted the inaugural address into a form that was adhered to by all presidents until Lincoln. These speeches attempt to articulate the president's understanding of republican principle. Many of them hardly allude at all to particular policy disputes, except as they can be deduced or extrapolated from the general interpretation of the Constitution. Jefferson, for example, tries to show "that the differences between the true party of Federalism and the true party of Republicanism is not a difference of principle and the principles of American government are shared by all true Republicans and Federalists."[42] Jefferson's interpretations of principles do, in fact, support many of his party's policies, but he attempts to mitigate party divisiveness by the form of his remarks.

Later presidents were more specific in their discussions of public policy. James Polk, for example, offered the most detailed list of policy objectives (prior to the Civil War), urging a lower tariff, no third Bank of the United States, and the annexation of Texas and Oregon.[43] However, the discussion of these topics is prepared by and emerges from an enumeration "of the principles which will guide me in the administrative policy of the government [that] is not only in accordance with the examples set by all my predecessors, but is eminently befitting the occasion." When Polk discusses the issue of tariffs, for example, he offers his thoughts in the context of his understanding of the meaning of the constitutional power "to lay and collect taxes, duties, and excises."

After the Civil War, the form of address was reversed. Presidents tended to enumerate policy concerns first, and then proceed to justify those policies in terms of vaguely articulated republican principles. The issues most frequently mentioned were (1) civil service reform, and (2) sound and stable currency and the payment of debts in spe-

---

[42] Ibid., 14. See also *Inaugural Addresses*, 12.

[43] For an enumeration of the major topics discussed in nineteenth-century addresses, see Edward W. Chester, "Beyond the Rhetoric: A New Look at Presidential Inaugural Addresses," *Presidential Studies Quarterly* 11, no. 1 (Winter 1981): 571–81. See also the introduction to Arthur Schlesinger, Jr., *The Chief Executive: Inaugural Addresses of the Presidents of the United States* (New York: Crown Publishers, 1965).

cie.[44] Many of these presidents did devote special attention to proposed constitutional reforms, and these provided an avenue to serious discussion of constitutional principle. Benjamin Harrison criticized the two-term presidency proposal, while Hayes proposed a six-year term. Harrison also suggested that the Secretary of the Treasury be independent of the president, and McKinley was critical of the thirteen-month "lame duck" congressional sessions between election and seating. Every president in the nineteenth century, except Zachary Taylor, mentioned the Constitution, and most of these addresses were at least partly structured by reflection upon its meaning. All of this was to change in the twentieth century. Symptomatic of the larger changes in form would be the fact that only half of the twentieth-century inaugural addresses even mention the word Constitution (or any of its provisions), and none of the twentieth-century addresses contain analyses of the meaning of the Constitution.

Proclamations

The other major "official" forms of popular communication in the nineteenth century were proclamations and executive orders. There is no strict division of the executive's "ordinance power" between executive orders and proclamations, but the general rule seems to have been (down to the present day) that proclamations pertain to matters of general or national concern, while executive orders are directed to parts (for example, individual exemptions from Civil Service rules, matters of administrative detail, etc.).[45] Of course, as students of government regulation would be quick to point out, narrow rules of executive orders may have important policy consequences, but for present purposes the character of proclamations is more interesting for what it reveals about the nineteenth-century understanding of popular leadership.

The first proclamation declared a day of thanksgiving and was is-

[44] Chester, "Beyond the Rhetoric," 575.
[45] James Hart, *The Ordinance-Making Power of the President of the United States* (Baltimore: Johns Hopkins University Press, 1925), 315–23.

sued by President Washington at the behest of Congress. In September of 1789, a joint committee of Congress waited on the president and presented him with Congress's resolution requesting him to recommend to the people a day of thanksgiving and prayer. The resolution did not specify the form that the president's "recommendation" should take. Washington adopted the form used by state governments, which themselves resembled "the form used by His Britannic Majesty."[46] This form, with insignificant emendations, has been preserved to the present day (although the extent and purposes of the use of proclamations have changed). These documents begin, "By the President of the United States of America, A Proclamation." This is followed by the preamble, which is a series of "whereas" statements (sometimes this "preamble" will be several pages long and ninety per cent of the text); then the body of the document begins ("Now therefore, I declare . . ."). Lastly, there is a formula of attestation, the signature of the president, and the countersignature of the secretary of state below the seal.[47]

The form of the proclamation virtually ensures that the central rhetorical appeal of any proclamation will be the authority of the president (or of the government as a whole) rather than factors peculiar to the president's persuasive abilities. Put another way, the proclamation's persuasive power derives more from the fact that the president proclaims, or commands, than it does from a case that he builds.

This rhetorical character is no more evident than in what is perhaps the most famous proclamation—Lincoln's Emancipation Proclamation. Lincoln simply declares "that on the first day of January, A.D. 1863, all persons held as slaves within any State . . . shall be then, thenceforward and forever free. . . ."[48] He does not justify his action in the proclamation. There is no case presented or brief upon the evils

[46] Hart, *Presidency in Action*, pp. 24–28; *Annals*, 1:949–50.

[47] Hart, *Presidency in Action*, p. 27. Hart details some of the subtle but important changes from British practice, including the replacement of the royal "we" with "I" in the declaratory sentence.

[48] James D. Richardson, ed., *A Compilation of the Messages and Papers of the Presidents, 1789–1897*, 10 vols. (Washington, D.C.: U.S. Government Printing Office, 1896–1899), 8:3358.

of slavery. (Richard Hofstadter once remarked that the Emancipation Proclamation "had all the moral grandeur of a bill of lading.")[49] Lincoln's example represents the pure case of the proclamation as command, although probably the typical case as well, in terms of its form (not gravity of issue).

However, some proclamations do contain an argument proper—an attempt to persuade. Standing at the opposite extreme from the Emancipation Proclamation is Andrew Jackson's proclamation nullifying an attempt by a state to assert the primacy of its law over the Union's. Jackson offers a detailed examination of the constitutional principle within an appeal to "Fellow Citizens" to think through "the momentous case" he has reviewed. For all the direct argument to the people, however, it is striking that Jackson seems prevented by the requirements of the form from attempting the blatant appeal to passion for which his oratorical abilities were reputedly well suited. Wishing to address the people on an issue of great moment, he does not, in fact, go to them directly, but rather indirectly, through a form—the only form permitted him by the governing doctrine of the time. The written form, along with the tone set by the particular demands of the "whereas . . . I declare" format, may have helped to raise Jackson's reflections to (or sustain them at) a level of deliberative speech.

The majority of proclamations in the nineteenth century did not address such serious issues. Most were hortatory and declaratory, like Washington's Thanksgiving Proclamation. Nevertheless, when important issues were communicated to the people, the proclamation served as the vehicle. In our time, momentous issues are more likely to be presented orally and visually in a context that makes the dramatic performance as important as the tangible text. For that reason, the use and significance of proclamations has changed considerably, even though their form remains the same.

The movement away from the formalism embodied by proclamations toward less structured informal speech gains support from the

[49] Richard Hofstadter, *The American Political Tradition* (New York: Knopf, 1948), 132.

most influential literature on the presidency today, or at least is reflected in that literature. Following Neustadt, most observers of the
presidency hold that a president's power to command depends upon
his power to persuade.[50] Without the power to persuade, so this reasoning goes, the formal authority promised by the Constitution will
not become actual. Certainly there is good sense to the notion that
commands are not, and never were, self-executing; they always require some background conditions that make authority possible. Re-
versing the emphasis of the current theory of leadership, the nineteenth-century presidents differ with Neustadt over the locus of those
authority-making conditions. Instead of command depending upon
persuasion, persuasion depends upon command. While command requires deference to authority, for nineteenth-century presidents that
is not achieved primarily by establishing "bargaining advantages,"
as it is for contemporary observers. Rather, deference to authority is
encouraged by the public articulation of constitutional principle by
the principal officers of the government and by the habitual attendance to form. Jackson's arguments, for example, carry with them a
weight that they could not have if he were not president, or if, while
president, he did not act like a constitutional officer.

This understanding of leadership is captured in a very oblique way
by the Court's opinion in the sole case dealing with the status of presidential proclamations, *Lapeyre v. United States*.[51] There, the issue
was whether a proclamation has to be published in order to have legal
effect. The proclamation in question was written on June 24, 1865,
but not published in newspapers until three days later. The Court held
that if the proclamation is written and sealed in the proper form, that
is enough for it to take legal effect—*it need not be heard* (or read) for

[50] See the discussion of Neustadt in Harvey C. Mansfield, Jr., "The Ambivalence
of Executive Power," in *The Presidency in the Constitutional Order*, ed. Bessette
and Tulis, ch. 9; see also Peter Sperlich, "Bargaining and Overload: An Essay on
Presidential Power," in *The Presidency*, ed. Aaron Wildavsky (Boston: Little,
Brown & Co., 1969), 168–92.

[51] 17 Wall. (U.S.) 191. See also Harvey C. Mansfield, Jr. "The Ambivalence of
Executive Power," 320–21.

its power to be binding; it need only be executed properly by a president.

Of course, in practice, proclamations may occasionally need to be supplemented with public reasoning (that is, with persuasion rather than the implied threat of coercion), and this may be so even when there is a reservoir of deference to presidential authority at the time of promulgation. In the nineteenth century, the sole "official" avenue for such public persuasion led through Congress, not to the people directly.[52]

Messages to Congress

Most of the messages to Congress were "Special Messages," written reports that generally confined themselves to a single issue. Often appended to a Special Message was a detailed technical report from an executive department. The Annual Message (now known as the State of the Union Address) and veto messages received the most scrutiny and were the most carefully crafted presidential remarks. As a group, messages to Congress were institutional devices suited to the demands of separation of powers and the president's role as co-partner in a deliberative process. To better understand the salient features of the nineteenth-century doctrine regarding popular leadership, consider the form and development of the Annual Message.

Washington's first Inaugural Address served also as his first Annual Message, and it established a short-lived precedent that was to become the subject of party controversy. Following British practice, the president received formal replies to his address from both houses of Congress. (In the House, James Madison chaired the special committee assigned to write the reply.) The two replies addressed each point of Washington's speech and thus constituted a kind of oath on the part of congressmen to do the virtuous deeds that Washington urged. The president received a committee of each branch of Con-

[52] A statistical overview of the various types of official rhetoric, displaying the marked differences between the nineteenth and twentieth century, is presented in Tables 5.1 to 5.5 in Chapter Five.

gress at the White House and replied to each reply, reading from a
written text.[53] (No accounts establish whether Washington prepared
his own remarks on the basis of an advance copy of the congressmen's, or whether he simply anticipated theirs.) The practice continued for all oral addresses by the president to Congress through the
John Adams administration.

Since "the custom was regarded as an English habit, tending to
familiarize the public with monarchical ideas," President Jefferson
abandoned the practice. Jefferson's main objection was to the oral
format, and the peculiar way that the president's physical presence
might affect the deliberative process. "I have had principal regard,"
he said, "to the convenience of the legislature, to the economy of
their time, to their relief from the embarrassment of immediate answers on subjects not yet fully before them, and to the benefits thence
resulting to the public affairs." Henry Adams shrewdly observes:
"The habit of writing to Congress was convenient especially to presidents who disliked public speaking."[54] Jefferson's practice of sending all messages to Congress in writing remained the rule until
Woodrow Wilson dramatically broke precedent with his appearances
before Congress.[55]

However sound Jefferson's argument against oral presentation, it
is not clear why "replies" are not more consistent with the republican principle than messages without them. Replies formally constituted a deliberative relation between the branches and offered the potential for the exercise of considerable legislative power. For this
reason, the abandonment of the practice was lamented in the early
nineteenth century by prominent congressmen, men who were re-
puted for their forceful criticisms of executive power.

John Randolph in 1809 suggested:

[53] *Annals*, 1:31–38, 241–42; Hart, *Presidency in Action*, 30–32.

[54] Henry Adams, *History of the United States During the Administration of
Thomas Jefferson*, 5 vols. (New York: Scribner's, 1889), 1:247–48. See also Noble
E. Cunningham, *The Process of Government under Jefferson* (Princeton, N.J.:
Princeton University Press, 1978), ch. 5.

[55] Wilson did *not* revive the practice of reply.

The answer to an Address, although that answer might finally contain the most exceptionable passages, was in fact the greatest opportunity which the opposition to the measures of the Administration had of canvassing and sifting its measures. . . . This opportunity of discussion of the answer to an Address, however exceptionable the answer might be when it had received the last seasoning for the presidential palate, did afford the best opportunity to take a review of the measures of the Administration, to canvass them fully and fairly, without there being any question raised whether the gentleman was in order or not; and I believe the time spent in canvassing the answer to a speech was at least as well spent as a great deal that we have expended since we discontinued the practice.[56]

In the midst of one of the most serious interbranch disputes in American history—the dispute arising from Jackson's "Protest" to the Senate—Daniel Webster reflected back upon the rhetoric of reply and contrasted its republican character favorably to Jackson's attempt to appeal to the people through Congress. In Webster's view, refraining from the rhetoric of reply gives much more support to monarchical designs than engaging in it.

Formerly, Sir, it was a practice for the President to meet both houses, at the opening of the session, and deliver a speech, as is still the usage of some of the State legislatures. To this speech there was an answer from each house, and those answers expressed, freely, the sentiments of the house upon all the merits and faults of the administration. The discussion of the topics contained in the speech, and the debate on the answers, usually drew out the whole force of parties, and lasted sometimes a week. President Washington's conduct, in every year of his Administration, was thus freely and publicly canvassed. He did not complain of it; he did not doubt that both houses had a perfect right to comment, with the utmost latitude, consistent with decorum, upon all his measures. Answers, or amendments to answers, were not unfrequently proposed, very hostile to his own course of public policy, if not sometimes bordering on disrespect. And when they did express respect and regard, there were votes ready to be recorded against the expression of those sentiments. To all this President Washington took no exception; for he well-knew that these, and similar proceedings, belonged to the power of popular bodies. But if the President were now

[56] Quoted in Adams, *History*, 248.

to meet with us with a speech, and should inform us of measures, adopted by himself in the recess, which should appear to us the most plain, palpable, and dangerous violations of the Constitution, we must, nevertheless, either keep respectful silence, or fill our answer merely with courtly phrases of approbation.[57]

Webster's remarks were made in a more general context of criticism of Jackson's attempt to appeal to the people through a communication to Congress, and he raises objections to popular appeals similar to those delineated in *Federalist* 49. The Senate, in fact, refused to officially "receive" the communication after reading it to the assembled body, for the reason that it was a popular appeal in the guise of an official communication. This fact indicates how well accepted the doctrine was at that time, but it conceals another point: Jackson was "forced" by the same doctrine to appeal to Congress in the first instance. The effect of this was to strip the "Protest" of any manifestly improper language or appeals to passion that could be easy marks for congressional censure. Indeed, in the lengthy debate that ensued (over a document that the Senate had already voted not to officially "receive" or publish in their Journal), several vigorous opponents of Jackson remarked that they could find no fault with his language, but instead with his conclusions and his motives.[58] Finally, this dispute, which began with a Senate resolution declaring that body's opinion that Jackson's bank policy was unconstitutional, evolved into a deep and serious discussion of the connection of the structure of the bureaucracy to the problem of executive accountability.[59] It would be hard to find a better example of a formal constraint fostering deliberation.

One measure of the distance between nineteenth- and twentieth-

[57] Daniel Webster, "The Presidential Protest," speech delivered in the Senate on May 7, 1834 (in Daniel Webster, *The Works of Daniel Webster*, 6th ed., 4 vols. [Boston: C. C. Little and J. Brown, 1853], 4:374).

[58] *Annals*, 10:1374.

[59] For contemporary use of the theories presented in Jackson and Webster's speeches, see Herbert J. Storing, "American Statesmanship: Old and New," in *Bureaucrats, Policy Analysts, Statesmen: Who Leads?* ed. Robert Goldwin (Washington, D.C.: American Enterprise Institute, 1980).

century politics in America is the careful attendance to forms and formalities in the former and the instinctive contempt for them today. The great French political scientist Alexis de Tocqueville detected the tendency of democracies to disregard formality while being the regimes most in need of them.

> Men living in democratic centuries do not readily understand the importance of formalities and have an instinctive contempt for them. . . . Formalities arouse their distain and often their hatred. . . .
>
> [T]heir chief merit is to serve as a barrier between the strong and the weak, the government and the governed, and to hold back the one while the other has time to take its bearings. Formalities become more important in proportion as the sovereign is more active and powerful and private individuals become more indolent and feeble. Thus democracies by their nature need formalities more than other peoples and by nature have less respect for them. This deserves most serious attention.[60]

Nineteenth-century presidents and their publics appreciated this insight more than their counterparts do today. As I indicate in the next chapter, their appreciation of the political importance of formality extended to ''unofficial'' or ''informal'' speech and behavior by presidents. The political story behind the formalities is not, as one might imagine today, the shrewd ways presidents got around them, but rather the power, political meaning, and democratic utility of formality itself.

[60] Alexis de Tocqueville, *Democracy in America*, ed. J. P. Mayer (New York: Doubleday, 1969), 698–99. For a commentary on this passage and reflection upon the status of forms today, see Harvey C. Mansfield, Jr., ''The Forms and Formalities of Liberty,'' *The Public Interest* 70 (Winter 1983): 121–31.

· 3 ·

THE OLD WAY:
DEVELOPED AND EXPRESSED

Washington, Adams, Jefferson, and Madison also established informal forms of rhetoric consistent with governing constitutional theory. The nineteenth-century presidents who followed differed in the degree to which this rhetorical ''common law'' was congruent with their particular political temperaments. Some—John Quincy Adams and Ulysses S. Grant, for example—were happy to shun virtually any public speech. Others, such as Pierce and McKinley, pushed against clearly perceived limits. Nevertheless, all of the administrations, with the striking exception of Andrew Johnson's, shared a core fidelity to the legitimate constraints of nineteenth-century constitutional theory.

Andrew Johnson did not adhere to the forms and doctrine of the nineteenth-century constitutional order. This single, seemingly aberrant case illustrates the power of the doctrine, because Johnson was formally and constitutionally challenged for his behavior on the stump. In the case of Johnson, one sees speech and constitutional text in political confrontation, revealing the power of one and the authority of the other. A discussion of this case concludes this chapter.

THE RHETORICAL PRESIDENCY

"Unofficial" Presidential Rhetoric

Because other nineteenth-century presidents might have appealed to the people unofficially in support of policy initiatives, even though official rhetoric, including inaugural addresses and other popular modes, remained consistent with basic doctrinal principles, inspection of "unofficial" nineteenth-century speech is necessary to determine its extent, its salient characteristics, and its principal purposes. One can see the power of forms if they serve to delimit or to formalize "informal" behavior as well as the conventional categories of political speech.

Yet if unofficial, where is this speech to be found? There are no official collections of unofficial speech. I canvassed three major sources for manuscripts or references to speeches: (1) the Library of Congress collections of nineteenth-century presidential papers, (2) private "unofficial" compilations of presidential speeches and addresses published in the nineteenth century, and (3) biographies of each of the nineteenth-century presidents. The quality of the manuscript collections varies from president to president, and the number and quality of biographies is also uneven, creating gaps in this set of data. However, by searching three major sources and by relying particularly upon biographies (which collectively numbered over sixty and drew upon hundreds of newspaper archives), one discovers those speeches which members of the culture themselves mark out as those which should be read.[1]

As might be expected, biographers differed in their judgment of incidents to report and in their assessments when reporting the same or very similar situations. However, these differences form a pattern

---

[1] Although Washington and Adams were presidents in the late eighteenth century, I refer to all presidents before Theodore Roosevelt as "nineteenth-century" presidents for ease of expression. "Nineteenth-century" signifies a congruence of ideas and practices, which is more important for my purposes than a designation of strictly historical time. Stephen Skowronek makes this issue of "political time" his theme, and presents demarcations different from mine, in "Notes on the Presidency in the Political Order," in *Studies in American Political Development*, vol. 1 (New Haven: Yale University Press, 1986), 286–302.

that corresponds to the doctrinal differences between the nineteenth and twentieth centuries. Biographers writing after 1930 about nineteenth-century presidents often omit references to popular speeches, judging them to be insignificant. More often, they tend to characterize those which are discussed as missed opportunities for forceful leadership of public opinion. Biographers writing in the nineteenth century (or educated in the nineteenth century and writing in the early twentieth century) are more likely to discuss popular speeches, to reproduce excerpts of them, and to consider the propriety of their presentation. For example, in 1960 Charles A. McCoy wrote, ''[James Polk] was handicapped by his complete inability to sloganize or to mobilize the public in behalf of his Administration by an appeal to emotion. . . . Try as he might to appeal to the masses, as was his wish in his fourth annual message, which he regarded as a valedictory address, he could not compress his views into a form suitable for mass consumption.'' In 1920, Eugene McCormack, on the other hand, depicted Polk as judiciously avoiding popular appeals because they contradicted the ''custom'' of the period; since such appeals would have involved a ''sacrifice [of] his dignity to beg in person for their support,'' their use might have worked to his strategic disadvantage. And although in 1899 Edward M. Shepard wrote a generally laudatory biography of Martin Van Buren, he understood and accepted Whig criticism of Van Buren's occasional departures from prevailing practice.[2]

I discovered approximately one thousand ''unofficial'' popular speeches delivered by nineteenth-century presidents. They are dwarfed in quantity by the tremendous number of direct popular appeals in our century. It would be a mistake to regard them as insignificant, however, for they yield insight into the legitimate and illegitimate functions of presidential rhetoric in the nineteenth century.

[2] Charles A. McCoy, *Polk and the Presidency* (Austin: University of Texas Press, 1960), 185; Eugene Irving McCormack, *James K. Polk: A Political Biography* (Berkeley: University of California Press, 1922), 144; Edward M. Shepard, *Martin Van Buren* (Boston: Houghton Mifflin & Co., 1899).

The Extent and Purposes of Popular Rhetoric

The extent of nineteenth-century presidential popular rhetoric is presented in Table 3.1. The first column gives the number of tours (sometimes called ''swings around the circle'') that presidents embarked upon specifically to see and address the people. The follow-

TABLE 3.1 Presidential Tours and Other Popular Communication, before the Twentieth Century

President	N of Tours	N of Speeches on Tour (est.)	N of Other Speeches (est.)	Total Speeches (est.)	Average N of Speeches per Year (est.)
Washington	2	20	5	25	3
Adams, J.	0	0	6	6	1
Jefferson	0	0	3	3	5
Madison	0	0	0	0	0
Monroe	2	40	0	42	5
Adams, J. Q.	0	0	5	5	1
Jackson	1	7	2	9	1
Van Buren	1	23	4	27	9
Harrison, W. H.	0	0	0	0	0
Tyler	1	5	0	5	1
Polk	1	15	0	15	3
Taylor	1	20	2	22	22
Fillmore	2	20	0	20	10
Pierce	2	19	1	20	5
Buchanan	1	8	1	9	2
Lincoln	0	0	78	78	16
Johnson	1	60	10	70	23
Grant	1	5	20	25	3
Hayes	6	126	0	126	31
Garfield	0	0	10	0	10
Arthur	1	25	15	40	10
Cleveland	1	25	36	51	6
Harrison, B.	3	281	15	296	74
McKinley	2	110	20	130	65

ing columns list estimates of numbers of speeches delivered on those tours, and of other speeches, addresses, and unofficial public communication for each president. Finally, since presidents served for different lengths of time, an estimated number of speeches per year is calculated for each president. The estimates include all of the speeches actually reported verbatim in whole or part (about half the total); those referred to in biographies; and others that could be presumed to have been made, given the character of the tour, the number of cities visited, and the president's normal routine as indicated by his activity in those cities for which we have complete accounts. It should be clear from the table that most of the popular speeches were made on tour. All remarks, however brief, are considered here as speeches, and it should be noted at the outset that perhaps 80 percent or more of these ''speeches'' were very brief ''thank-you'' remarks to welcoming greetings given the president.

There was a substantial increase in speechmaking after the Civil War, which raises questions about treating the century as a unit. The discussion of forms and purposes that follows will show that there were important developments or changes within the century, and that some presidents (such as Hayes, Benjamin Harrison, and McKinley) appeared in public quite often. Nevertheless, the activity of these presidents was fundamentally similar to that of their predecessors and fundamentally different from twentieth-century practice after Woodrow Wilson.[3]

In addition to an increasing amount of popular rhetoric, there was some change in its purposes or functions after the Civil War. Table 3.2 presents a broad picture of the variations and changes in purposes. Each mark indicates that a president pursued that purpose even if only one speech could be found fitting the designation. Clearly the categories overlap; some speeches served several func-

[3] One may speculate that since the character of popular speech did not change as much as its quantity, the development of the railroad rather than a major doctrinal shift accounts for the rise in the amount of speechmaking toward the end of the century. The train permitted presidents to visit many cities, sometimes several states, in one day.

TABLE 3.2 Purposes of Popular Presidential Rhetoric

President	1	2	3	4	5	6	7	8	9	10
					Purposes					
Washington		x	x	x	x	x	x			
Adams, J.		x				x				
Jefferson		x				x				
Madison	x									
Monroe		x		x	x	x				
Adams, J. Q.		x	x		x					
Jackson		x	x		x	x				
Van Buren		x		x	x		x		x	
Harrison, W. H.	x									
Tyler		x	x		x					
Polk		x	x		x					
Taylor		x	x							
Fillmore		x	x		x	x	x			
Pierce		x	x	x						
Buchanan		x				x	x			
Lincoln		x	x	x	x	x	x	x		x
Johnson		x		x		x	x		x	x
Grant		x	x		x					
Hayes		x	x	x			x			
Garfield		x	x	x						
Arthur		x	x	x						
Cleveland		x	x						x	
Harrison, B.		x	x	x	x	x	x			x
McKinley		x	x	x	x	x	x			

KEY: 1 = no popular rhetoric
    2 = greetings, "thank you" for welcome
    3 = speech associated with a ceremony (e.g., dedication of monument)
    4 = patriotic exhortation
    5 = reassurance by presence, attempt to *gather* information (sometimes referred to by presidents as "seeing and being seen")
    6 = attempts to establish peace and harmony among the regions or sections of the nation
    7 = articulation of general policy direction of administration (e.g., with regard to "economy," "foreign policy," etc.)
    8 = defense of war policy or action
    9 = identification of president's position as partisan (i.e., a position adopted by an organized, named political party)
   10 = attack on defense of a specific legislative proposal (or set of proposals) before Congress

tions. The table is intentionally biased toward overestimation of the intended functions of popular rhetoric in order to reinforce the claim of limited use of popular rhetoric in the century.

The purposes are placed in a progression from no discussion of the "issues of the day" to discussion of specific policy proposals or laws. As the decrease in marks towards the right side of the table illustrates, the more policy-oriented a speech, the less likely it was to be given in the nineteenth century. Only four of twenty-four presidents attempted to defend or attack a specific bill or law. Only two presidents made a partisan speech (meaning one that aligns itself with the views of an organized party). Strikingly, only Lincoln discusses war. Madison and Polk do not even deliver speeches to rouse the spirit of soldiers or citizenry in time of war, let alone to defend their policies. Finally, only nine presidents articulated the general policy direction of their administrations in a popular format.

The historical survey below illustrates more fully the few general and specific policy statements that were made in order to show how even they differed from contemporary practice. As in the discussion of "official" rhetoric, analysis of rhetorical practices amplifies the meaning, and confirms the political dominance, of the nineteenth-century doctrine.

Presidents and Popular Rhetoric

George Washington seldom delivered speeches or addresses to the people. Yet his few popular addresses, made mainly on well-publicized tours, set the tone for most unofficial rhetoric that followed. The first president also received many petitions, letters of congratulation or concern, and requests for assistance from the citizenry. In response to a few of these he published replies—a written form that came to be known as "Replies to Addresses."[4] Washington's replies simply iterated patriotic sentiment; later presidents used replies for more substantive purposes. By writing these replies, Washington conformed to the constitutional injunction to speak infrequently and

---

[4] For examples of some of Washington's "Replies" see James Hart, *The American Presidency in Action: 1789* (New York: Macmillan Co., 1948), 21–24.

also retained discretion in picking those to whom he would reply. These features of his practice maintained the integrity of his deliberative duties as well as the executive quality of flexibility.[5]

Washington's most famous popular communication was the Farewell Address. Originally composed by Madison for use at the close of Washington's first term, the text was rewritten by Hamilton, and edited by Washington at the end of his second term. In its original draft, Felix Gilbert says, "Madison had woven together a justification of Washington's decision to retire, a praise of the American Constitution and an exhortation to preserve the advantages of the Union." The final text was intended to articulate the constitutional principles more concretely, so that they might actually influence future conduct and, more particularly, justify a certain broad direction for foreign policy. Historians have been primarily concerned with the extent to which Hamilton "repudiated" Madison through his rewriting or to show how subtle changes of argument reflected partisan disputes at the time of construction. To some extent the latter activity is a continuation of elite correspondence that circulated at the time of the Address. For our purposes, several obvious features of the address are noteworthy: it was a written form of address that rose to a high level of deliberative expression—argument characteristic of *The Federalist*, for example; it was published without any ceremony, relying upon the force of its argument and the authority of its author to persuade; finally, it attempted to provide policy direction that was Federalist, to be sure, but that was presented in a mode that covered or mitigated partisan differences. The fact that historians, like Kremlinologists today, have to examine the document with extreme care in order to find hints of partisanship is indicative of the power and constraint of the form of address adopted.[6]

[5] Washington declined to reply to Quaker addresses against the slave trade, "on the ground that he might have to act officially [later]," James Southall Freeman, *George Washington*, 6 vols. (New York: Charles Scribner's Sons, 1954), 6:252.

[6] Felix Gilbert, *To the Farewell Address* (Princeton, N.J.: Princeton University Press, 1961), 121, 115–36; see also Victor Hugo Paltsis, ed., *Washington's Farewell Address* (New York: New York Public Library, 1935).

Washington also established the practice of "going on tour." He took two of these journeys, one to New England and the other through the South. Washington revealed two prime purposes for the travels: to gather information, particularly concerning the "temper and disposition of the people toward the new government," and to ease any tensions that might have existed between regions. For these purposes, public speaking was not as important as public appearances—"seeing and being seen," as Washington called them. The *Gazette of the United States* wrote that the president's appearance would eradicate any "uneasiness" that might exist in the South and that "seeing him . . . will have a very conciliatory effect, and do more than a thousand arguments from even an Ames or a Gerry (considered the two most effective orators in Congress)." The president did give speeches on those tours, but they contained general articulations of republican sentiment, not even a clear enunciation of principle. Reflecting upon the southern tour Washington wrote, " . . . It has enabled me to see with my own eyes the situation of the country through which we traveled, and to learn more accurately the disposition of the people than I could have done by [written] information. . . . Tranquility reigns among the people, with that disposition towards the general government which is likely to preserve it. . . ." Washington established the function of "seeing and being seen" and with it a tendency to treat tours as auxiliary to the president's narrowly executive function of carrying out the law and preserving tranquility, rather than his legislative responsibility to initiate new policy.[7]

John Adams continued Washington's practice of occasionally mingling with the people, holding levees and tea parties each week at the White House. However, he embarked on no tours and gave only "thank-you" greetings to groups that honored him with dinner when he travelled to Quincy, Massachusetts to vacation or that sent him "addresses" of support. (Exasperated by Adams's failure to popularly defend his policies, which biographer Gilbert Chinard be-

---

[7] Freeman, *Washington*, 6:240, 322; letter of July 20, 1791, to David Humphreys, quoted in Freeman, *Washington*, 6:321.

lieved to be correct, Chinard wrote: "Had [Adams] been younger or more willing to address the people directly and explain his policies, Adams would . . . have had the chance to go before the country as the man who had kept America out of war and who, between French and British intrigues, had steered a strictly national course.") Adams's only speeches of any extent were made when he met with delegates of Indian tribes and made formal remarks that were translated to the tribesmen, a practice begun by Washington and perfected by Jefferson.[8]

Thomas Jefferson held three meetings with tribal representatives, and later Andrew Jackson hosted a famous meeting with a delegation of Choctaw Indians. Still later in the century, Abraham Lincoln made a speech to delegates from several tribes. None of the presidential biographers makes clear whether the treatment of the Indians as different from either foreign nations or domestic "interest groups" was ever discussed. What is clear is that presidents regarded these meetings as part of their constitutional responsibility to enforce treaties and to preserve domestic tranquility. It is never stated, but may be plausibly suggested, that Indians were spoken to rather than sent a written "reply" so that they could be accommodated in three ways: First, these ceremonies resembled Indian ritual in meetings between tribes. There may have been a fear of offending the Indians by dictating the form of discourse. Second, there may have been a desire to avoid any misapprehension of meaning by retaining the ability to immediately amend, or more fully explain, a statement. Finally, since the major complaint of the Indians was the failure by settlers to respect treaty commitments, there may have been the desire to publicly embody or show respect as a mode of public education.

Jefferson offered no popular communications other than these meetings with Indian delegations. He preferred to supplement direct messages to Congress with private communication (letters, meetings, etc.).[9] It is remarkable that the early president known most for

[8] Gilbert Chinard, *Honest John Adams* (Boston: Little, Brown & Co., 1933), 300; Page Smith, *John Adams*, 2 vols. (New York: Doubleday, 1962), 2:962.

[9] Of course, many of these private communications were leaked to the press. How many leaked documents were intended to be leaked is impossible to estimate. Du-

his democratic views spoke the least to the people directly. Perhaps even more remarkable is that James Madison followed Jefferson's practice of public silence, relying on proclamations as his mode of direct communication with the people, in the face of the need for public-spiritedness and resoluteness during the War of 1812.[10]

James Monroe, however, reinstituted the "tour," making two journeys, one in 1817 to New England and another in 1819 to the South and West. His declared purpose was to inspect forts and defense preparations as commander-in-chief. He added to Washington's purposes of "seeing and being seen" and encouraging harmony among the states and regions, a more particular interest "to create an occasion for the Federalists to demonstrate their loyalty to the national government in a public way, and thereby hasten the process of party amalgamation."[11] Most of Monroe's replies to addresses made to him on the tour were oral (though several were written after the tour and sent to those who had honored him). In all the instances of which we have record, the rhetoric took the form of an exhortation to rise above faction or party. As he stated after inspecting the site of Fort Trumbull:

> Believing that there is not a section of our union nor a citizen who is not interested in the success of our government, I indulge a strong hope, that they will all unite in the future, in the measures necessary to secure it. . . . I indulge a strong hope, and even entertain great confidence, that our principle dangers and difficulties have passed, and that the character of our deliberations, and the course of the government itself, will become more harmonious and happy, than it has hitherto been.[12]

mas Malone, *Jefferson and His Times*, 5 vols. (Boston: Little, Brown and Co., 1974), 5:146. See also the chapter on Jefferson in Norman J. Small, *Some Presidential Interpretations of the Presidency* (Baltimore: Johns Hopkins University Press, 1930).

[10] Madison did anonymously pen several "stern anti-French editorials for the *National Intelligencer*" (Ralph Ketchum, *James Madison* [New York: Macmillan Co., 1971], 536).

[11] Harry Ammons, *James Monroe: The Quest for National Identity* (New York: McGraw-Hill, 1971), 371.

[12] S. Putnam Waldo, *The Tour of James Monroe, President of the United States,*

One twentieth-century proponent of popular leadership laments, "[D]espite his unprecedented opportunity to talk directly with the people, Monroe never referred, even in passing, to the issues of the day. There was nothing in these speeches to suggest that the President had a program for the nation, that he was interested in bills before Congress, or even that he wanted popular support for his foreign policy. Always he stressed unexceptionable 'republican principles' and the revolutionary inheritance."[13]

Despite his career as a teacher of rhetoric at Harvard, where he authored *Lectures on Rhetoric and Oratory*, John Quincy Adams chose to retreat even from the limited direct rhetoric of Monroe. He did mingle with the people, opening the White House on New Year's Day to receive "everybody high and low, friend and foe, and who wished to offer compliments of the season if not good wishes for the coming year."[14] Two to three thousand people showed up in 1827. Yet Adams refused to embark on any tour, making only perfunctory greetings and toasts to small gatherings in 1827 after attending his father's funeral, and a fifteen-minute address congratulating builders and townsfolk at the groundbreaking of the Chesapeake and Ohio Canal. According to Samuel Flagg Bemis, "John Quincy Adams never liked to 'exhibit himself to the people.'" Declining an invitation to address the Maryland Agricultural Society, Adams wrote to the Society's secretary that it would cost him four precious days' work and set a precedent for other unnecessary excursions. "See thou a man diligent in *his* business. . . . From cattle shows to other public meetings for purposes of utility or exposures of public sentiment, the transition is natural and easy."[15] Adams avoided contact with his supporters and with the people at large on his trips to vacation despite the urgings of his wife, who suggested that there was a

---

Through the Northern and Eastern States in 1817 (Hartford, Conn.: Silas Andrus, 1820), 158.

[13] Stuart Gerry Brown, *The American Presidency: Leadership, Partisanship, and Popularity* (New York: Macmillan Co., 1966), 11–12, 124.

[14] Samuel Flagg Bemis, *John Quincy Adams and the Union* (New York: Alfred Knopf, 1965), 98.

[15] Ibid., 99.

wide difference between courting and shunning the advances of the public. On one occasion, a trip to Baltimore, Adams did propose a prepared toast, "adapted from Voltaire's Le blanc et le noir: 'Ebony and Topaz': General Ross's coat of arms and the republican militiaman who gave it." The toast was so obscure (and so rare a public pronouncement) that it provoked both jokes of derision and "overinterpretation" by the sophisticates.[16] Martin Van Buren wrote, "I can perceive neither sense nor wit in the President's toast unless (which can scarcely be possible) he meant by Ebony and Topaz to personify the Slave and Free states. Can that be? He is fond of obscure but bitter allusions." This incident is an example of a problem that emerged in nineteenth-century practice. So rare was popular rhetoric for some presidents that isolated forays into the genre sometimes took on a significance well beyond that apparently intended. Or, if searching interpretation was intended, the president lost control of it by his brevity.[17]

Andrew Jackson may have been beset by similar difficulties. Known as an ardent democrat, a "leader of the people" by his followers and a demagogue by his critics, it is striking that, like Jefferson, Jackson rarely gave speeches. He did meet with Indian chiefs on one occasion, and proposed another overinterpreted toast on another ("Our federal Union, it must be preserved").[18] His reputation as a

[16] Ibid., 101.

[17] Martin Van Buren to C. C. Cambreleng, October 22, 1827, quoted ibid., 101. "The only public address Adams made as President was on the occasion of the breaking ground for the Baltimore and Ohio Canal, July 4, 1828" (ibid., 102). Earlier he had turned down an invitation to a similar event claiming, "I am highly obliged to my friends for their good opinion; but this mode of electioneering [to celebrate the opening of the Pennsylvania Canal] is suited neither to my taste nor my principles. I think it equally unsuitable to my personal character and to the station in which I am placed." Josiah Quincy, ed., Memoirs of John Quincy Adams (Boston: Philips, Sampson and Co., 1859), 158.

[18] On the controversy surrounding the toast see Marquis James, Andrew Jackson: Portrait of a President (New York: Bobbs Merrill, 1937), 232–33. The speech to representatives of the Choctaw Indians was conciliatory and stands in marked contrast to his private utterances while president and public pronouncements earlier. See also Michael Paul Rogin, Fathers and Children (New York: Alfred Knopf, 1975).

popular leader derives not from his activities as a popular speaker but from his attempt to address the people *through* the Annual Message, the Nullification Proclamation, and the "Protest" to Congress, and from his informal but effective support of the administrative information organ—a newspaper dedicated to publishing the president's policy positions.[19] One should not overlook these developments. There may be some merit to William Graham Sumner's complaint: "It was a new mode of statement for the President to address Congress, not on his own mention, and to set forth his own opinions and recommendations, but as the mouthpiece of 'a large portion of our fellow citizens.' Who were they? How had they made their opinions known to the President? Why did they not use the press or the Legislature as usual. . . . What becomes of the constitutional responsibility of the President?"[20] As significant as this transformation of practice by Jackson is, Sumner and other historians have not noted the other side of the story. Jackson's disposition was unlike that of Adams. He liked popular speaking and did much of it before becoming president. But once in office, he was constrained by a set of settled practices. Forced to put his case "before the people" in a message to Congress, the deliberative character of the address was raised above what it might have been had it been delivered directly, orally, to a mass audience.[21]

The effect of doctrine as constraint is even more clearly revealed in the character of Jackson's tour. This "popular leader" had to forego politics on the issue of the removal of the bank deposits when he went on tour. As Arthur Schlesinger, Jr. states, "The campaign for removal [of the bank deposits] slowed down in May and June, during the President's trip to New York and New England." Jackson's most

---

[19] The reputation also derives, in part, from reports of iconoclastic remarks made by Jackson in private meetings. See Arthur Schlesinger, Jr., *The Age of Jackson* (New York: Book Find Club, 1945), 365.

[20] William Graham Sumner, *Andrew Jackson* (Boston: Houghton Mifflin and Co., 1882), 103.

[21] To get a sense of what the counterfactual speech might have produced, note the contrast between Jackson's written messages and Andrew Johnson's oral addresses which I discuss below.

74

famous communication to the people was the Nullification Proclamation, and again, as discussed previously, the form structured and constrained the appeal. Schlesinger notes, "[T]he mass of the people . . . slept over [most of the] passages while responding unreservedly to the central appeal—the preservation of the Union."[22]

Jackson's successor, Martin Van Buren, was the first president to attempt to break free of the constraints of prevailing practice. Although he gave no significant public speeches or addresses for three years, he did attempt to turn a sentimental tour from Washington, D.C. to his hometown in New York State into a campaign for a second term. Received by huge crowds in New York City, Van Buren began his remarks to the Mayor and assembled guests, "I am cheerfully and gratefully affected by this cordial reception by my Democratic Fellow Citizens of New York City and County of New York."[23] Singling out Democratic listeners was the extent of his partisanship, but it provoked a storm of protest. At three of the towns on his tour, Troy, Schenectady, and Hudson, Whig politicians on the governing councils managed to pass resolutions declining to receive the President of the United States because of the impropriety of the one sentence that I quoted from his New York City speech. The rebuke at Hudson was particularly stinging. Van Buren had begun his career there, but before he arrived, the "city of his adoption" adopted a resolution censuring him and his rhetoric.

> It is therefore plain—beyond the power of argument to make it plainer, that Mr. Van Buren's tour is one of a political and partizan character.—Therefore be it
>
> Resolved, by the Mayor and Common Council in the city of Hudson, in Common Council assembled, that we do not feel bound by any consideration of *justice, prudence,* or *hospitality,* to expend the people's money, or descend from the dignity of our official stations, for the purpose of aiding political partizans in their endeavors to carry out their favorite schemes.[24]

[22] Schlesinger, *Jackson*, 96–98.

[23] Martin Van Buren, *Papers of Martin Van Buren*, microfilm (Washington, D.C.: Library of Congress, Manuscript Division), Reel 15.

[24] Denis Tilden Lynch, *An Epoch and a Man: Martin Van Buren and His Times* (New York: Horace Liveright, 1929), 432.

The Common Council's action raised the curiosity of the citizenry in surrounding counties. "Many thousands" of them journeyed to Hudson to hear the president. If they had come to hear the sort of speech that was censured, they must have been disappointed. While the people were enlivened, the president was chastened. After "the cannon had roared a Presidential salute," Van Buren spoke briefly. "There was no suggestion of politics in his utterances. . . ."[25] Reaching his birthplace of Kinderhook the following day, Van Buren discarded a draft partisan address for an extemporaneous autobiographical account of the local boy who became president. While Van Buren apparently succeeded in "founding" a party system, he did not succeed in establishing popular partisan rhetoric as a form of presidential leadership.[26]

Van Buren's successor, William Henry Harrison, died after one uneventful month in office. John Tyler, who succeeded Harrison, and who attempted to found a third party in 1844, gave no significant public addresses. Indeed, on tour in the summer of 1843, the main speaker at several receptions was someone other than the president. The most notable speech of the tour was Daniel Webster's oration at Faneuil Hall, Boston, in commemoration of the completion of the Bunker Hill Monument. Attendance at this event was the stated purpose for the entire tour, yet the president made only one of numerous "toasts" there.[27]

Like Madison some years earlier, James Polk, president during the Mexican War, gave surprisingly few speeches. He embarked upon one tour, but we have been unable to locate any copy of the speeches made then (though it appears that he delivered several). Although he

[25] Ibid. See also Holmes Alexander, *The American Talleyrand: The Career and Contemporaries of Martin Van Buren, Eighth President* (New York: Harper & Brothers, 1935), 358–59.

[26] Lynch, *Martin Van Buren*, 433. On Van Buren "founding" a party system, see James W. Ceaser, *Presidential Selection: Theory and Development* (Princeton, N.J.: Princeton University Press, 1979), ch. 3, and Marvin Meyers, *The Jacksonian Persuasion* (Stanford, Calif.: Stanford University Press, 1957), appendix B.

[27] Oliver Perry Chitwood, *John Tyler: Champion of the Old South* (New York: Appleton Century, 1939), 319–23.

and his wife "attended a few balls and now and then made a personal appearance at a trade convention or some other event . . . he was rarely seen by the general public . . . he was troubled when he was forced to leave his office to attend art showings, college commencements and similar affairs. And he thought time spent in public to be 'time unprofitably spent.' "[28]

Zachary Taylor continued the laconic mode of leadership. He even further narrowed one hitherto acceptable function of the presidential tour. Embarking on a tour of the northeast in the summer of 1849, Taylor declared "his purpose . . . to see that section of the country, its people, and its need, that he went to see, *not* to be seen, and had no desire for public receptions."[29]

Millard Fillmore became president when Taylor died in office. He revived a more active role for popular leadership without violating the norms of the nineteenth-century doctrine. Accepting an invitation to speak at ceremonies commemorating the completion of the Erie Railroad, "Fillmore turned the ceremonies into a gala peace demonstration." As an auxiliary device to "faithfully execute the law," Fillmore gave short speeches in which he defended the Compromise of 1850 and urged that prosperity could only come with "sectional peace."[30] Fillmore was the first president since Washington to discuss general policy in his popular communications (and Washington had limited his discussion to a single written Farewell Address). Fillmore's policy talks were after the fact—that is, they did not intrude upon the deliberative process. Rather, they were a tool consistent with the narrow notion of an executive as one who carries out the law.

Franklin Pierce followed Fillmore's presidency and his practice, and even ventured into an oblique discussion of prospective policy.

[28] Bill Severn, *Frontier President: James K. Polk* (New York: Ives Washburn, Inc., 1965), 157; see also McCoy, *Polk*, 185.

[29] Brainerd Dyer, *Zachary Taylor* (Baton Rouge: Louisiana State University Press, 1946), 401 (my emphasis).

[30] Robert J. Rayback, *Millard Fillmore* (Buffalo, N.Y.: Buffalo Historical Society, 1959), 289.

On tour, Pierce limited his own speeches to discussion of the compatibility of the Union with states' rights and a general endorsement of free trade as consistent with republicanism. The principle theme ''iterated and reiterated with many illustrations from the Revolutionary War was the 'glory of the Union!' '' But with Pierce on the tour were several members of his cabinet. These associates ventured into more specific discussions of policy. Secretaries David and Guthrie endorsed the then-popular proposal for rail transportation to the Pacific. ''They were to make the practical speeches and leave the President the Union and American ideals.''[31]

James Buchanan abandoned even Pierce's restricted use of policy rhetoric by Cabinet members, offering only ''greetings'' on tour and making no other public speeches, except one ''Farewell Address'' during the 1860 election campaign. However, Buchanan did carry on a ''vast [private] correspondence'' that both reiterated and strengthened his convictions with regard to Republican ''wickedness'' during the 1856 Congressional campaign.[32] The one public speech that he did deliver was a political address, that criticized the Democratic Party's nominating procedure, endorsed Breckenridge, and defended the principles that property is a matter of definition for separate states and that majority rule should prevail in the territories.[33] The speech reflected the crisis of the critical election that the country was about to face, and the freedom from constraint that a lame-duck president might feel. It was extemporaneous in form and, unlike Washington's Farewell, not carefully crafted. Nevertheless, it appeared to be constrained by a tradition of constitutional argument. Buchanan reviewed Supreme Court decisions and articulated an understanding of constitutional principle that supported Chief Justice Taney's views in *Dred Scott*. While his conclusions were, like Ta-

[31] Ray Franklin Nichols, *Franklin Pierce: Young Hickory of the Granite Hills* (Philadelphia: University of Pennsylvania Press, 1958), 281.

[32] Elbert B. Smith, *The Presidency of James Buchanan* (Lawrence: University of Kansas Press, 1975), 6.

[33] The speech is printed in George Ticknor Curtis, *Life of James Buchanan*, 2 vols. (New York: Harper and Bros., 1883), 2:290–95.

ney's, bad constitutional interpretation, and immoral as well, they are well presented and relatively free of overt appeal to passion.

Abraham Lincoln not only arrested and changed the course of policy begun by Buchanan, he repudiated the style of leadership embodied by Buchanan's farewell speech. As his train headed East to the Inauguration, Lincoln greeted thousands, but in speech after speech he repeated the sentiment expressed in the passage quoted here in Chapter 1—that he could not discuss the issues of the day extemporaneously, that they would have to await a "proper" occasion. Lincoln's speech on "silence" was probably his typical speech, so often did he make it.[34]

I have suggested that most of the presidents in the nineteenth century were constrained by settled practices and the doctrine behind them. It should be apparent that the depth of understanding of the doctrine varied from president to president, however consistent a particular president's behavior might be with the doctrine. As might be expected, Lincoln not only offered his rhetoric in forms consistent with the doctrine, he also reflected upon the doctrine, and his reflections can expand ours.

Several of Lincoln's greetings developed beyond the obligatory expression of appreciation to a discussion of the rationale behind his silence. Five basic reasons for silence were offered. First, Lincoln expressed his own lack of "wisdom" prior to the Inauguration. He needed time to assess situations about which he had little firsthand knowledge. Premature discussion might be transparently foolish or commit the nation to a foolish course. Time would allow for education and careful construction of his remarks. "Others will agree with me that when it is considered that these difficulties are without precedent, and have never been acted on by any individual situated as I am, it is most proper that I should wait, see the developments, and get the light I can, so that when I do speak authoritatively I may be

[34] *Collected Works of Abraham Lincoln*, ed. Ray P. Basler, 9 vols. (New Brunswick, N.J.: Rutgers University Press, 1953–55), 4:201–202, 206, 209, 210, 216, 219, 221, 222, 226, 230.

as near right as possible.''[35] Second, Lincoln wished to await developments, not only to understand them, but that they might ''work themselves out.'' He could not yet assess the significance his intrusion would have. In this context, he suggested a need to ''restrain ourselves,'' and warned that raising passions, even without intending to do so, would be ''particularly dangerous.'' Third, Lincoln urged that he would eventually take a stand he believed to be ''right.'' On his understanding of right, such a stand would admit of little hedging or change once taken.[36] Silence thus allowed for flexibility as well as wisdom. Fourth, Lincoln noted, ''In my present position it is hardly proper for me to make speeches. Every word is so closely noted that it will not do to make trivial ones, and I cannot be expected to be prepared to make a mature one just now.''[37] Some have suggested that the rhetorical presidency might be a reflection of increased *opportunity* for popular leadership (development of wire services, mass communications, etc.), rather than a doctrinal change. Lincoln makes clear not only that he did not lack opportunity, but that such opportunities were the problem. Hastily formed statements might engender a course of policy that was unintended. Finally, Lincoln indicates that ''silence'' will enhance the persuasive power of those speeches that he does deliver. Stressing the need to make his pronouncements on ''proper'' or authoritative occasions, Lincoln recognizes the need to rest his authority on the Constitution rather than upon raw popular will. For popular will is transient, and may be the object upon which authority might have to be brought to bear. To the extent that the Constitution is recognized by the citizenry to be the authority that it is, Lincoln's pronouncements would be more effective, especially if the immediate occasion for them was unpopular.[38]

I have kept silence for the reason that I supposed it was peculiarly proper that I should do so until the time came when, according to the customs of the country, I should speak officially [Voice, partially in-

[35] Ibid., 4:221.
[36] Ibid., 4:210–211.
[37] Ibid., 5:450.
[38] Ibid., 4:231.

terrogative, partially sarcastic, "Custom of the country?"], I heard some gentleman say, "According to the custom of the country"; I alluded to the custom of the President elect at the time of taking his oath of office. That is what I meant by the custom of the country. . . . And now, my friends, have I said enough? [Cries of "No, no," "Go on," etc.] Now my friends there appears to be a difference of opinion between you and me, and I feel called upon to insist upon deciding the question myself. [Enthusiastic cheers.]"[39]

Authoritative speech combines the power of command with the power of persuasion (or force of argument). Lincoln wished to provide the conditions for effective command by focusing the citizenry's attention on carefully crafted rhetoric presented "officially." Moreover, after such addresses (e.g., First and Second Inaugurals, Messages to Congress, Emancipation Proclamation) Lincoln often refused to amend or embellish his statements in popular settings, referring the audience back to the original text. For example, in reply to a "Serenade" in Honor of the Emancipation Proclamation, Lincoln said: "What I did, I did after very full deliberation, and under a very heavy and solemn sense of responsibility. . . . I shall make no attempt on this occasion to sustain what I have done or said by any comment."[40]

Of Lincoln's seventy-eight popular speeches and addresses, by far the largest group of these (forty-five) consisted of greetings to delegations, army groups, remarks from the platform of his train, etc. It was on these sorts of occasions that Lincoln expressed his views on keeping silent. He also often iterated his purposes to see and be seen ("I have stepped out upon this platform that I may see you and you may see me, and in the arrangement I have the best of the bargain") and to reinforce patriotic sentiment ("Standing as I do, with my hand upon this staff, and under the folds of the American flag, *I ask you to stand by me so long as I stand by it*").[41]

Lincoln's policy positions were normally expressed in his official

[39] Ibid., 4:231. See also, 5:358, 5:438, 5:450, 7:302.
[40] Ibid., 5:438.
[41] Ibid., 4:218, 220, 222, 223.

rhetoric. However, on several occasions he developed the principles of his position in a popular mode. The important point to note is that each of these speeches was self-consciously constrained by the demands of constitutional argument. In response to a Serenade, the president urged passage of the constitutional amendment to abolish slavery.[42] He did this *after* the amendment had passed congressional scrutiny, and he indicated the reasons why his Emancipation Proclamation needed to be supplemented. His most famous public utterance, of course, was the Gettysburg Address. In addition to its intention to articulate constitutional principle, not to defend a bill or specific policy, it should be noted that Lincoln was scheduled as the second speaker at those ceremonies, that the importance of the speech derives from the care with which it was composed and from the extent to which it transcended the exigencies of its time to reinterpret the origins and ends of American politics. Despite this radical objective, perhaps because of it, the central rhetorical claim of the Gettysburg Address repeats that of his "typical" speeches on silence: Lincoln contrasts necessary deeds with unnecessary words.[43]

Lincoln's last public speech articulated the principles on which he wished reconstruction to proceed. In this speech he makes it clear that an immense practical difficulty exists regarding the reintegration of the South into the Union. He urges encouragement for the new government of Louisiana, which has "sworn allegiance to the Union . . . adopted a free state constitution . . . and voted to ratify the [anti-slavery] constitutional amendment recently passed by Congress. . . ." Lincoln's speech appears to be peculiarly and inextricably related to his executive function of ensuring domestic tranquility, though to be sure, that function overlaps with the legislative one of determining a general policy toward the South. Finally, even in

[42] Ibid., 8:254.

[43] For the most thorough analyses of the argument of the Gettysburg Address, see Glen E. Thurow, *Abraham Lincoln and American Political Religion* (Albany: State University of New York Press, 1977) and Eva T. H. Brann, "The Gettysburg Address," in *Abraham Lincoln and the Gettysburg Address*, ed. Leo Paul de Alvarez (Dallas: University of Dallas Press, 1978).

this last speech, Lincoln several times says that he will not discuss a topic currently the subject of legislative dispute.[44]

Lincoln's most specific policy pronouncements are those in which he justifies war activity after the fact.[45] The most important of these are his defenses of suspension of habeas corpus and of martial law in two replies to addresses. Carefully choosing written arguments made to him, he too responds in the written form of a public letter. These documents are extraordinary for both their detail and their power of argument. The rationale for them is never explicitly discussed by Lincoln, but two features make them consistent with the general doctrine. First, as indicated above, they were written, not spoken. Second, they discussed actions Lincoln had taken on his own initiative (without prior consent of Congress), and they were addressed to those affected by such action. With respect to the last point, it should be noted that since Lincoln based his justification of these extraordinary measures upon a Lockean understanding of "prerogative," he was compelled to realize, as Locke did, that the "ultimate appeal" in such unusual situations is to the people.[46]

Lincoln's crisis and his policies were extraordinary. Given those facts, it is striking that his rhetoric adhered to the doctrinal prescriptions of his time. His speeches are certainly the best known of all of American political oratory. Their influence and their effect might be connected to the fact that, looking at the whole of Lincoln's activity, he gave relatively few popular addresses. Lincoln refused to cloud the discussion of first principles with prolix pronouncements.

On the other hand, delivering about seventy policy speeches on the stump, President Andrew Johnson violated nearly every element of

[44] Basler, *The Collected Works of Lincoln*, 8:399–405.

[45] The one "before the fact" discussion of policy other than the final reconstruction speech occurred in a meeting on the problems and prospects of recolonization with a delegation of black leaders. Congress had appropriated "a sum of money" for the purpose, and Lincoln wished to assess its feasibility. How public his remarks were at the time is unclear, however. Ibid., 5:371.

[46] Ibid., 6:260, 300. John Locke, *The Two Treatises of Government*, ed. Peter Laslett (New York: New American Library, 1960), ch. 14.

the nineteenth-century doctrine. Johnson is a clear exception, and a discussion of his rhetoric will close this chapter.

President Grant issued no significant public statements during his presidency. Like other post-Civil War presidents who had been officers in the Union Army (Hayes, Garfield, Benjamin Harrison, and McKinley), Grant occasionally gave "greetings" at Grand Army of the Republic reunions. Grant refused to publicly participate in his own campaigns of 1868 and 1872 and declined to publicly support fellow partisans at the mid-term elections (although he did aid them privately).[47]

Rutherford B. Hayes revitalized the tour, using the train to reach over one hundred cities and towns on several journeys. While Hayes delivered over one hundred speeches, nearly all were brief greetings and urgings of a "larger spirit of fraternity and conciliation and national unity." Charles Williams notes that the contemporary press focused upon his policy silence in light of the fact that "the public prints were ringing with discussion . . . of his treatment of the South." On three or four occasions Hayes discussed economic policy at length, less to articulate the merits of a particular program than to indicate that his overall direction was consistent with republicanism. At the end of the tour to the West in 1880, on election eve, Hayes offered his sole public political endorsement. It was "too late now to enter upon a political discussion," he told Republicans of the county, but then went on to urge election of James A. Garfield.[48]

While James Garfield had broken precedent with an extemporaneous "front porch" campaign for office that was unusual in its references to current events, once president he delivered no significant addresses. In several brief addresses in the summer of 1881 he "resolutely avoided political subjects."[49] Garfield was assassinated later

[47] See William B. Hesseltine, *Ulysses S. Grant, Politician* (New York: Unger Publications, 1935).

[48] Charles Richard Williams, *The Life of Rutherford Birchard Hayes* (Boston and New York: Houghton Mifflin Co., 1914), 2:242, 297; see also Harry Bainard, *Rutherford B. Hayes and His America* (Indianapolis: Bobbs Merrill, 1954), 494.

[49] Theodore Clarke Smith, *The Life and Letters of James Garfield*, 2 vols. (New Haven, Conn.: Yale University Press, 1925), 2:1031.

that year. His successor, Chester A. Arthur, confined his speechmaking to brief greetings with no policy content at ceremonial functions (e.g., the centennial of Yorktown, dedication of the Washington Monument, etc.).[50]

The last three presidencies in the nineteenth century constitute a transition period. While Teddy Roosevelt doggedly pursued a strategy of appealing to the people regarding specific legislative matters, and Woodrow Wilson supplied the doctrinal justification for such activity, the late-nineteenth-century presidents flirted with the idea but failed to pursue a consistent popular strategy. They neither lacked physical opportunity nor technical means to conduct new political practices. Yet without a coherent theory to provide political legitimacy, they could not articulate a truly new rhetoric.

Grover Cleveland refused to be drawn into active campaigning and followed the example of Tilden, Hayes, and Garfield in keeping aloof from the "hurly-burly," but he did make two campaign speeches on civil service reform, tax reduction, and the needs of labor. Once in office, however, Cleveland confined his policy rhetoric to formal messages to Congress. While he would occasionally make an off-the-cuff comment on tour that would receive much attention in the press, Cleveland's speeches themselves were generally "local in character" and incidental to unimportant ceremonial occasions. Twentieth-century historian Allan Nevins lamented, "Whoever introduced [this style of speech], it was not happy. Cleveland would have done well to avoid these pedestrian discourses, and to intersperse several carefully written speeches upon national policy with a number of informal talks." Cleveland did, however, publish collections of his correspondence year by year in an effort to foster a climate favorable to his party's policies. One letter, accepting his party's nomination in 1888, was an explicit appeal to the people and a restatement of his party's platforms.[51]

[50] George Frederick Howe, *Chester A. Arthur: A Quarter Century of Machine Politics* (New York: Dodd Mead, 1934), 247.

[51] Allen Nevins, *Grover Cleveland: A Study in Courage* (New York: Dodd Mead,

Benjamin Harrison, who became president after Cleveland's first term (but was succeeded by Cleveland), attempted to introduce policy discussion into the tour. Most of these speeches were still of the "greeting" type; many expressed the sentiment that the occasion was not appropriate "to give you some information on the State of the Union . . . and to make some suggestions, as to what would be wise [policy]."[52] Yet Harrison did discuss several matters pending before Congress—railroad safety regulation and postal service bills, for example. The most interesting feature of Harrison's rhetoric on these sorts of occasions was his hesitance. Some indications of this hesitance come close to expressions of guilt at violating a norm he knew he should respect. For example:

> [At a Chamber of Commerce reception at which he endorses the suggestions of a previous speaker regarding national defense and economic policy:] "I . . . will not enter into any lengthy discussion here. Indeed, I am so careful not to trespass upon any forbidden topic, that I may not in the smallest degree offend those who have forgotten party politics in extending this greeting to us, that I do not know how far I should talk upon these public questions."[53]
>
> [At a very large reception in Omaha, Nebraska, where he discusses need for foreign markets and for a sounder dollar:] "But, my countrymen, I had not intended to speak so long. I hope I have not intruded upon any ground of division."[54]
>
> [At Kingston, New York:] "You ask for a speech. It is not very easy to know what one can talk about on such an occasion as this. Those topics that are most familiar to me, because I am brought in daily contact with them, namely, public affairs, are in some measure prohibited to me. . . ."[55]

Harrison allowed himself to be drawn into extemporaneous policy discussion against his professed better judgment. His successor, Wil-

---

1934), 318, 320; see also Robert McElroy, *Grover Cleveland*, 2 vols. (New York: Harper and Bros., 1923), 2:234–35.

[52] Benjamin Harrison, *Speeches of Benjamin Harrison*, comp. Charles Hedges (New York: U. S. Book Co., 1892), 246.

[53] Ibid., 383.

[54] Ibid., 469.

[55] Ibid., 495.

liam McKinley, proceeded in an opposite fashion. McKinley announced to associates an intention "to make a series of speeches on behalf of the tariff-reciprocity treaties, which the administration had negotiated with several foreign countries but on which the Senate had as yet failed to act." However, the speeches emerged as general discussions of the requisites of prosperity and make no mention of pending bills or treaties. There is no speech that even alludes to the Spanish-American War, the sinking of the Maine, the problem of "Jim Crow" laws, or United States policy toward the Philippines, all major issues faced by McKinley.[56] Indeed, much of McKinley's rhetoric was characteristic of the century as a whole: expressions of greeting, inculcations of patriotic sentiment, attempts at building "harmony" among the regions of the country, and very general, principled statements of policy, usually expressed in terms of the policy's consistency with that president's understanding of republicanism.

THE GREAT EXCEPTION: ANDREW JOHNSON

. . . they talk about impeachment. So far as offenses are concerned—upon this question of offenses, let me ask you what offenses I have committed? [A Voice—"Plenty, here, to-night."]
    —President Andrew Johnson on Tour, St. Louis, 1866[57]

President Andrew Johnson's popular rhetoric violated virtually all of the nineteenth-century norms encompassed by the doctrine. He stands as the stark exception to general practice in that century, so

[56] Lewis L. Gould, *The Presidency of William McKinley* (Lawrence, Kans.: Regents Press, 1980), 244; "Remarks of the President at McComb City, Mississippi," May 1, 1901, *Papers of William McKinley*, microfilm (Washington, D.C.: Library of Congress, Manuscript Division), file 14; "Remarks at Surf, California," May 10, 1901, *McKinley Papers*, file 44; "Speech at Citizens' Banquet," Memphis, Tennessee, April 30, 1901, *McKinley Papers*, file 10. See also Margaret Leech, *In the Days of McKinley* (New York: Harper and Bros., 1959), 341, 408, 575.

[57] Eric L. McKitrick, *Andrew Johnson and Reconstruction* (Chicago: University of Chicago Press, 1960), 438.

demagogic in his appeals to the people that he seems not so much a forerunner of twentieth-century practice as a parody of popular leadership. As we shall see, Johnson's exceptional behavior supports the interpretation of the "rule" of nineteenth-century doctrine. He was warned away from his rhetoric by his advisers, chastised in the press of his own time, and ultimately censured (though not convicted) by congressmen, whose impeachment charges included one for the bad rhetoric used on tour to gain support for his reconstruction policies.

Johnson's best-known speeches were two responses to Serenades at the White House, and eleven (of about sixty) speeches delivered on a nineteen-day tour to win support for his policy toward the South. All of these speeches were, in fact, variations on one speech. Like contemporary electoral campaigns, Johnson had one rough outline, carried in his head, on which he rendered variations for particular audiences. In the typical speech, Johnson would begin by disclaiming an intention to speak, proceed to invoke the spirits of Washington and Jackson, claim his own devotion to the principles of Union, deny that he was a traitor as others alleged, attack some part of the audience (depending on the kinds of heckles he received), defend his use of the veto, attack Congress as a body and single out particular congressmen (occasionally denouncing them as traitors for not supporting his policies), compare himself to Christ and offer himself as a martyr, and finally conclude by declaring his closeness to the people and appealing for their support.[58]

Most of these speeches were impassioned. Their vituperativeness varied according to the audience. As Eric McKitrick has pointed out, "Andrew Johnson was essentially a stump speaker rather than a polished orator." His effectiveness depended on a continual "communion with the audience," an interplay with hecklers, and the spiritedness and vitality characteristic of effective extemporaneous talk.[59]

[58] Ibid., 292–94, 428–36; see also James David Barber, "Adult Identity and Presidential Style: The Rhetorical Emphasis," *Daedalus* 97, no. 3 (Summer 1968):938–68.

[59] McKitrick, *Johnson and Reconstruction*, 429; Barber, "Adult Identity and Presidential Style," 942–48.

Nothing could be further from the founders' intentions than for presidential power to depend upon the interplay of orator and crowd. This interplay may or may not persuade the immediate audience, but the effect of such activity upon the president's office, upon his dignity, upon his future ability to persuade, and upon the deliberative process as a whole is likely to be deleterious. Such was the case for Andrew Johnson.

In his first Serenade, delivered on Washington's birthday to a crowd gathered outside the White House, Johnson accused his congressional opposition of being just as treasonable as "the Davises and Tombeses, the Slidells, and a long list of others" from the South during the war. A voice called, "Give us the names."

> A gentleman calls for their names. Well, suppose I should give them. . . . *I say Thaddeus Stevens, of Pennsylvania* [tremendous applause] *I say Charles Sumner* [great applause] *I say Wendell Phillips and others of the same stripe among them* [A Voice—"Give it to Forney"]. Some gentleman in the crowd says, "Give it to Forney." I have only to say that *I do not waste my ammunition* upon dead ducks. [Laughter and applause.][60]

Johnson went on to accuse his opponents of plotting to assassinate him. It is in this context that he offers himself to the people as a Christ. "If my blood is to be shed, let it be shed. . . . But let the opponents of the government remember that when it is poured out 'the blood of martyrs shall be the seed of the Church.' " Johnson was to repeat this theme again and again on tour. Accused in the press of playing not Christ but Judas Iscariot, Johnson publicly responded: "The twelve apostles had a Christ, and he never could have had a Judas unless he had twelve apostles. If I have played the Judas, who has been my Christ that I have played the Judas with? Was it Thad Stevens? Was it Wendell Phillips? Was it Charles Sumner?"[61]

These remarks and twenty or thirty more passages like them were seized nationwide by the press (which was dominated by the radical

---

[60] McKitrick, *Johnson and Reconstruction*, 294. Italics and audience reaction in the original.

[61] Ibid., 432.

opposition to Johnson). As the tour progressed, opposition hecklers came prepared, knowing that the president would deliver "the speech." Johnson relied more and more upon the novelty produced by audience interaction rather than upon alternative sets of arguments. There is some dispute among historians regarding Johnson's effectiveness in persuading his immediate hearers. Some allege him to have "converted" hostile crowds, while others depict him as merely inflaming the divisions before him, or in some instances alienating potential supporters in his midst. But *all* of the major studies of the period agree that Johnson's tour was ineffective—indeed, counterproductive for his own efforts, as news of his actions spread throughout the nation. One contemporary who had supported Johnson and his policies before the tour put the point this way:

> President Johnson, in his speech at Cleveland, remarked that "he did not care about his dignity." In our judgment this is greatly to be regretted. The American people care very much about it and can never see it forgotten without profound sorrow and solicitude. . . . The President of the United States cannot enter upon an exchange of epithets with the brawling of a mob, without seriously compromising his official character and hazarding interests too momentous to be thus lightly imperiled.[62]

Johnson's own Cabinet and advisers echoed those sentiments. Several Cabinet members refused to go on tour with him. His friend Senator Doolittle of Wisconsin warned him not to be drawn into extemporaneous speeches, to say nothing "which had not been most carefully prepared beyond a simple acknowledgment."[63] And "on Monday, February 24, 1868, the House of Representatives of the Congress of the United States, resolved to impeach Andrew Johnson, President of the United States, of high crimes and misdemeanors, of which, the Senate was apprised and arrangements were made for trial." Johnson's improper rhetoric not only solidified his opposition, it served as the basis for the tenth article of impeachment:

---

[62] Ibid., 438. See also Lloyd Paul Stryker, *Andrew Johnson: A Study in Courage* (New York: Macmillan, 1929), 341–72, and James E. Sefton, *Andrew Johnson and the Uses of Constitutional Power* (Boston: Little, Brown & Co., 1980), 140.

[63] Barber, "Adult Identity and Presidential Style," 948.

That said Andrew Johnson, President of the United States, unmindful of the high duties of his office and the dignity and propriety thereof . . . did . . . make and deliver with a loud voice certain intemperate, inflammatory, and scandalous harangues, and did therein utter loud threats and bitter menaces as well against Congress as the laws of the United States. . . . Which said utterances, declarations, threats, and harrangues, highly censurable in any, are peculiarly indecent and unbecoming in the Chief Magistrate of the United States, by means whereof . . . Andrew Johnson has brought the high office of the President of the United States into contempt, ridicule, and disgrace, to the great scandal of all good citizens.[64]

The impeachment charge of bad and improper rhetoric has received little notice in the writings on impeachment, and on the reconstruction period, probably for three reasons. First, the Tenure of Office Act issue was the basis for ten of the eleven articles of Impeachment; second, many congressmen participating in the proceedings were skeptical that "bad rhetoric" constituted an impeachable offense; and finally, due to the unreflective acceptance of popular leadership in our time, the few scholars who have noted the charge assume it must have been "frivolous."[65] But the significant fact is that no congressman expressly disagreed with the opinion that Johnson's rhetoric was improper, undignified, and damaging to the presidency. But for the legal argument that such activity was not a "high crime or misdemeanor," the only other argument offered by congressmen in Johnson's defense was that he was not drunk when giving the speeches, as Johnson's opponents had alleged. And among those congressmen reluctant to press the charge, many based

[64] U.S. Senate, *Proceedings in the Trial of Andrew Johnson* (Washington, D.C., 1869), 1, 4, 5–6.

[65] See, for example, Louis Fisher, *Constitutional Conflicts between Congress and the President* (Princeton, N.J.: Princeton University Press, 1985), 154; Michael Les Benedict, *The Impeachment and Trial of Andrew Johnson* (New York: W. W. Norton, 1973), 144; John R. Lobovitz, *Presidential Impeachment* (New Haven: Yale University Press, 1978), 63–64. Compare this observation by one of Johnson's leading opponents: "In 1867 the question of the impeachment of Andrew Johnson began to be discussed. Indeed, its discussion was in large part rendered possible by his performances in a western tour in advocacy of his own election. They disgusted everybody." Benjamin F. Butler, *Butler's Book* (Boston: A. M. Thayer & Co., 1892), 926.

their opinion on strategic considerations (whether the defense could delay the trial) rather than upon a judgment that the charge was improper.

The major proponent of the "bad rhetoric" charge was one General Butler, a man whose past hindered the sober consideration of his arguments. Butler was a famous public speaker known for his own bursts of demagoguery. Yet Butler rightly pointed out that impeachment could better be defended on the grounds of public harangues than on violation of the Tenure of Office Act—a technical charge that ran counter to the resolution of most removal controversies of the past. Said an impassioned Butler:

> . . . we have only presented to the Senate and country the bones and sinews of the offenses of Andrew Johnson. I want to clothe those naked bones and sinews with flesh, enliven them with blood, and show him as he is, the living, quivering sinner that he is, before this country. Why, Sir, hereafter, when posterity shall come to examine the proceedings of this day, if they read only the articles which we have heretofore presented [covering the Tenure of Office Act], they will wonder why, even with so good a case as we have upon mere questions of technical law, we undertook, without other provocation, to bring this prosecution against a good and great man, as the President, without other proof or allegation, ought to be presumed to have been.[66]

Butler rested his case on two precedents drawn from impeachments of sitting judges (Chase and Humphreys) accused of making inflammatory harangues. It was objected that while the judges made their harangues from the bench, in their official capacities, Johnson made his on tour and in unofficial, off-the-cuff remarks. Butler rightly responded: "But a judge exercises his office only while on the bench, while the President of the United States can always exercise his office, can exercise it wherever he may be. He can never divest himself of that high character."[67]

The president never goes on recess; his residence is his official office, whether it be the White House or his vacation retreat, because

---

[66] *Congressional Globe*, 40th Congress, 2nd Session (March 3, 1868), 1640.
[67] Ibid., 1641.

the chief executive is in an official capacity all of the time. Given that fact of executive power, the Johnson case illustrates the difficulty of maintaining the distinction between official and unofficial rhetoric.

Andrew Johnson's experience also illustrates the power of rhetorical forms as political constraints. A number of scholars have suggested that Johnson's rhetorical failure stemmed from problems of self-esteem or perhaps a deep and serious psychological sickness. Johnson turned to popular rhetoric, argues James David Barber, in order to feel the kind of approbation from the crowd that he could not elicit elsewhere in his life. Whatever the psychological explanation for Johnson's motive, the fact remains that a political system may be structured to be hospitable or inhospitable to such political activity, and a political culture may be taught to approve or disapprove of it. In the present case, Johnson's speeches as senator were very different from those as president, even though, according to Barber, Johnson's character was basically the same throughout his adult life.

> Sometimes he could give a calm address; most of his speeches in the Senate, for example, were reasoned arguments, more like a lawyer's brief than a stump harangue. But as his performance on the Swing Around the Circle made clear, he repeatedly—almost uniformly—burst forth in fiery rhetoric whenever he faced a crowd of partisans.[68]

But the constraints of form remain effective only so long as there is a doctrine to give them legitimacy. Johnson renamed the tour his "Swing around the Circle." In his time the name became a topic of derision, the subject of political cartoons, the symbol of the failure that was Johnson's. For the rest of the nineteenth century, tours were called tours and were much closer in character to Washington's and Monroe's initial journeys than to Johnson's. While it is safe to surmise that Johnson's fiery demagoguery would be considered improper even today, the *purpose* of his speech, to rouse public opinion in support of his policy initiatives in Congress, illegitimate in his time, has become acceptable, even commonplace, in ours.

[68] Barber, "Adult Identity and Presidential Style," 949.

· 4 ·

THE MIDDLE WAY:
STATESMANSHIP AS MODERATION

In the changing use of language one can sometimes notice the altered status of legitimate rule. At the turn of the century, Theodore Roosevelt embarked upon a series of rhetorical campaigns to secure passage of legislation to regulate the railroads. He did not hesitate to describe these tours as ''swings around the circle''—the same label that signified the discredited practice that impeached Andrew Johnson. Roosevelt could use Johnson's phrase because he appropriated the arguments of Johnson's opponents to defend his activity. If popular rhetoric was proscribed in the nineteenth century because it could manifest demagoguery, impede deliberation, and subvert the routines of republican governance, it could be defended by showing itself necessary to contend with these very same political difficulties. Appealing to the founders' general arguments while abandoning some of their concrete practices, Roosevelt's presidency constituted a middle way between the statecraft of the preceding century and the rhetorical presidency that was to follow.

Between two understandings of the presidency's place in the polity, Roosevelt offers us an extraordinary perspective upon the constitutional order. Looking back upon the nineteenth century, Roosevelt can see problems that accompany the delimitation of presidential leadership. Looking forward to our time, Roosevelt's thought reveals the dilemmas that attend leadership's routinization.

Roosevelt's best-known and most important "swings around the circle" were on behalf of legislation that came to be known as the Hepburn Act of 1906. This legislation delegated power to the Interstate Commerce Commission to regulate railroad shipping rates and to maintain and enforce compliance with those regulations. Roosevelt's campaign for this Act and the principle behind it came to represent or symbolize his whole domestic policy. Roosevelt called his policy "the square deal," naming a principle he believed could mediate the claims on behalf of and against wealth.[1] For Roosevelt, the label "square deal" would summon consideration of a principle of fairness—an idea formed and enunciated prior to its advertisement in this catchy phrase.

Nearly all subsequent presidents would define their administrations in similar terms: The New Freedom, The New Deal, The Fair Deal, The Great Society, The New Federalism, and WIN ("Whip inflation now," Gerald Ford's unintentional parody). But after the first Roosevelt, only Woodrow Wilson would be as self-conscious in the articulation of his principles and their relation to the demands of popular leadership. We now take for granted what Roosevelt experienced as fresh and new. As leadership through capsulization would become routine, it would become an expectation—and as an expectation it would structure as much as service presidential policy.[2]

Theodore Roosevelt's "middle way" was, in fact, a campaign for

[1] Theodore Roosevelt, *The Roosevelt Policy*, ed. William Griffith, 2 vols. (New York: The Current Literature Publishing Co., 1919), 1:252.

[2] It is worth noting that the most popular presidents since the second world war—Eisenhower and Reagan—have not labeled their overall policies and in this respect resemble presidents of the nineteenth century.

See Fred I. Greenstein, *The Hidden Hand Presidency* (New York: Basic Books, 1982), and James W. Ceaser, "The Theory of Governance of the Reagan Administration," in *The Reagan Presidency and the Governing of America*, ed. Lester M. Salamon and Michael S. Lund (Washington, D.C.: The Urban Institute Press, 1984), 57–90.

moderation—moderate use of popular rhetoric, moderate appeals for moderate reform (that did not socialize but merely regulated industrial capitalism), and most importantly, an appeal to moderate disputes that Roosevelt feared might anticipate and signal class antagonism severe enough to prompt civil war.

To break precedent as decisively—which is to say as extremely—as Roosevelt did in the service of moderation is the most general of several ironies that characterize his statesmanship. In this chapter I explore why he tried to use popular rhetoric against popular rhetoric, why he denounced demagoguery demagogically, and why he formed an alliance with his opposition party on a matter of utmost importance to his own party. To justify these tactics, Roosevelt had to step outside of the constitutional order to see it whole. To understand Roosevelt's statesmanship and its importance to American political development, we have to recover his systemic perspective.

Can the lessons of Theodore Roosevelt's statecraft be embodied in a constitutional order and taught to subsequent presidents? Or does any attempt to institutionalize this sort of discretionary "personal" power transform and subvert that very power? Can one construct a political order that encourages extreme tactics and moderate policy, or must institutions necessarily be biased against extreme tactics if they are to tend to moderation in result? The story of Theodore Roosevelt's campaign for the Hepburn Act illustrates the ambivalence of the rhetorical presidency.

THEODORE ROOSEVELT AND THE HEPBURN ACT

In his Annual Message to Congress, delivered in December of 1904, Theodore Roosevelt urged the legislature to draft a law that would stop railroads from providing discriminatory rebates for large shippers, and to empower the Interstate Commerce Commission to set maximum allowable railroad rates in order "to keep the highways of commerce open to all on equal terms. . . . The government must in increasing degree supervise and regulate the workings of the railways engaged in interstate commerce; and such increased supervision is the only alternative to an increase of the present evils on the one hand or a still more radical policy on the other."[3]

The House of Representatives quickly passed the Esch–Townsend Bill in February 1905, but the Senate killed it in committee. One concession to emerge from the Senate committee, however, was a commitment to hold extensive hearings on the issue during the spring. Two months were given over to this technical and difficult subject, and a five-volume record thousands of pages long was produced. The report of the hearings was so extensive that there later arose a dispute over the cost of publishing them. While the Senate hearings proceeded, Roosevelt campaigned for a railroad bill on a "swing" through the middle west and southwest, en route to a Rough Riders reunion in Texas. Speeches in Dallas, San Antonio, Denver, and Chicago received extensive coverage in the press. A series of commencement speeches and other addresses later that summer continued the campaign. And in early fall, Roosevelt embarked upon another "swing" through the southeast en route to a visit to his mother's family in Georgia, speaking in Richmond, Raleigh, Charlotte, Atlanta, and Little Rock. His rhetorical campaign culminated with an Annual Message to Congress in December that devoted its first eighteen pages to railroad rate regulation.

In January, Iowa Congressman Peter Hepburn introduced his bill, and again, the House quickly passed the regulatory legislation at the beginning of February. The House vote was overwhelming (346 yea; 7 nay; 29 not voting, 3 present). The bill was referred to the Senate Commerce Committee, where Jonathan Dolliver, a Republican from Iowa, prepared to lead the fight for it. But the majority leader of the president's own Republican Party, Nelson Aldrich, was vehemently

---

[3] *Presidential Addresses and State Papers of Theodore Roosevelt*, 4 vols. (New York: P. F. Collier & Son, n.d.), 3:133–34. In this section, I rely upon the crisp legislative history presented in David M. Chalmers, *Neither Socialism nor Monopoly* (Philadelphia: J. P. Lippincott Co., 1976); John M. Blum, *The Republican Roosevelt*, (Cambridge, Mass.: Harvard University Press, 1954); Henry F. Pringle, *Theodore Roosevelt* (New York: Harcourt, Brace, 1931); and especially *Congressional Record*, 59th Congress, First Session, 1906, Volume 40.

opposed, along with the president's close friends, Henry Cabot Lodge and Philander Knox. ''Virtually all the most influential newspapers of the country were also opposed to it. The prevailing opinion in press and public was that the measure would never pass the Senate.''[4]

Aldrich succeeded in taking away management of the bill from Dolliver, giving it instead to a Democrat, ''Pitchfork'' Ben Tillman of South Carolina. ''Ben Tillman's vituperative race-baiting had done little to endear him even to many southerners of his own party.''[5] This demagogue had not been on speaking terms with the president since the Senate had censured him for brawling in the Senate chamber four years earlier. Tillman had no love for a president who claimed in a magazine article that the senator ''embodied retribution on the South for having failed to educate the cracker, the poor white,'' or a president who also took delight in claiming that Tillman's brother ''had been frequently elected to Congress on the issue that he never wore an overcoat or an undershirt.''[6]

By placing ''that serpent-tongued agrarian as its guide, the bill could not be labeled 'Republican.' For Dolliver, this was a staggering personal blow; for Aldrich, a beguiling triumph; for Roosevelt, an embarrassing problem. . . .''[7] Aldrich hoped to force Roosevelt to seek support from Democrats, and further divide and alienate his own party. Tillman surprisingly rose to the task, illustrating the founders' proposition that an institutional station could elevate a man of low motives and questionable character. The South Carolinian adopted a statesmanlike demeanor in the Senate and, for a time, achieved practical accommodation with the president, who dealt with him through intermediaries. For his part, the president, who once said, ''When I'm mad at a man I want to climb right up his

[4] Joseph B. Bishop, *Theodore Roosevelt and His Time*, 2 vols. (New York: Charles Scribner's Sons, 1920), 2:1.

[5] Chalmers, *Neither Socialism nor Monopoly*, 22.

[6] *Review of Books* (September 1896), quoted in Mark Sullivan, *Our Times: The United States 1900–1925*, 3 vols. (New York: Charles Scribner's Sons, 1930), 3:231.

[7] Blum, *Republican Roosevelt*, 95.

chest," reconciled himself to the situation, claiming that he didn't "care a rap" who got credit for a good bill as long as it was a good bill. "I was delighted to go with [Tillman] or with any one else just so long as he was traveling my way—and no longer."[8]

The debate on the floor of the Senate lasted eleven weeks. Dolliver supplied some of the thoughtful defenses of the bill for Tillman, while Aldrich relied upon the acumen of Senators Foraker (of Ohio), Lodge, and Knox. The status of private property in the regime and the economic consequences of governmental interference motivated the partisans of big business and of the railroads, of course. Yet discussion on these large themes quickly transformed itself in Senate debate into disputes over the constitutionality of the delegation of power to the ICC and over the intended scope of judicial review of ICC findings.

Opinion on the latter issue dominated the debate and divided into three camps. Aldrich and his followers pressed for review broad enough to allow the courts to rescind all or any commission actions, to rehear evidence presented in administrative proceedings, and to suspend ICC enforcement until the conclusion of litigation. Fearful that the courts, well known in the nineteenth century for their protections of capital, would render the ICC impotent to act, Tillman and his supporters advocated legislation that would explicitly restrict judicial review to determinations of whether the ICC had exceeded its authority. Dolliver staked out a middle position: that the courts should themselves determine the scope of review based upon their understanding of judicial power inherent in the Constitution.

Roosevelt waited several months before committing himself to one of these positions. In April, convinced that with the president's support, Tillman could forge a bipartisan coalition with twenty-six *Democratic* votes, Roosevelt endorsed the narrow review stance, providing Tillman with an amendment drafted by his attorney general. However, Tillman's coalition appeared to be one vote short when the Democrats caucused, so Roosevelt shifted his position and

[8] Sullivan, *Our Times*, 232. Theodore Roosevelt, *Theodore Roosevelt: An Autobiography* (New York: Macmillan Co., 1913), 475.

supported the moderate Republican position of Dolliver, supplying him with another amendment drawn by the attorney general. He did so without informing Tillman who, feeling betrayed, resorted to some of the oratorical flourishes for which he had become famous. Dolliver and Roosevelt persuaded one of Aldrich's supporters, Senator William Allison, to sponsor the amendment, which provided for judicial review but left it up to the the the Court to decide its scope. On May 18, 1906, Roosevelt's bill was passed into law by an exceptionally large majority, with only three senators voting against it.

The Hepburn Act gave the ICC the power to replace maximum rates; to supervise private cars, switching facilities, and other arrangements with big business; to forbid special passes for favored customers; to impose a triple-damage penalty for rebating; and to require and audit uniform accounting systems.[9] In the following decade, the Supreme Court considered the scope of judicial review under the law, refused to rehear the evidence upon which the commission made its decisions, and established for itself, in essence, Tillman's narrow review of statutory or constitutional authority. It would not be unreasonable to suggest that the Hepburn Act gave birth to the modern administrative state.

CONDITIONS OF SUCCESS

Defeated in 1904 on this issue, opposed by the leadership of his own party, allied to a partisan for whom he had nothing but contempt—how did Roosevelt do it? How did he win, and win so decisively? No answer to this question could be fully satisfactory, because with only one case it is difficult to isolate the peculiar features or to assess their weights in contributing to victory. If one cannot establish precisely the forces of political success, one can nevertheless discuss the configuration of these conditions or characteristics which appear together relatively rarely in American political history, and which call

---

[9] Chalmers, *Neither Socialism nor Monopoly*, 25.

attention to analogous characteristics in the very few later presidential triumphs. Formally, the conditions that were remarkable in this political success were: 1) the character of the issue; 2) the salience of the issue; 3) the quality of the president's legislative skills; and 4) the character and quality of the president's rhetorical skills.

The Issue

Although railroad regulation resulted from an interest group battle to secure material reward in a commercial economy, the character of the issue is not best described in strictly economic terms. Railroad regulation was perceived to be a moral issue that raised a number of politically constitutive questions, including the meaning of privilege, wealth, social standing, corruption, and conspiracy in a republican regime. For this reason, railroad regulation had as much to do with—perhaps more to do with—the reaffirmation and reinterpretation of American political principles as with material readjustment per se. For Americans, railroad regulation raised questions about the meaning of a regime that encouraged economic gain—that is, about the principles upon which the pursuit of economic gain is based.

This deeply political dimension of the dispute was addressed forthrightly by Roosevelt in his speeches, which I will discuss below. Because on first glance these issues appear to be, if not technical, at least more sophisticated than normal citizen concerns, one wonders why this policy engaged average Americans. Why did railroad regulation prompt fundamental, regime-level debate, since most political disputes, if pushed far enough, could raise the same sorts of concerns? Why not, say, oil regulation, or banking regulation? Why did railroad regulation so galvanize the public's attention, and provide Roosevelt with considerable leverage in the Congress? Part of the answer, of course, is simply that Roosevelt made this an issue. But he claims to have focused upon it because it already was a public concern, and historians seem to agree. It was a deep public concern, I think, because it summoned powerfully negative symbols. These symbols derive their power from characteristics peculiar to railroad-

102

ing as an industry or to the history of the railroad industry in America, and they mark this issue as exceptional, if not unique.

For example, the fundamental question of the relation of rich and poor is raised dramatically by an industry that divides at the same time that it connects. It may be no accident that "the other side of the tracks" has become a synonym for poverty, or that "railroad" has become a verb meaning "to push through without due process." The physical division that railroads embodied was accompanied by the simultaneous enrichment of some and impoverishment of others as towns flourished or died according to their proximity to the railroad. Unlike most public utilities, the railroad established service according to class, "first" or "second."

The belief that railroad companies formed the center of a vast conspiracy on the part of huge corporations was supported not only by the fact that it was often true, but also by the physical representation of the railroad system itself—a vast network of arteries connecting the nation's parts to each other. Business interconnections with railroad companies resembled the routes of the railways where complicated switching was visible to all who ventured to the next town.

As railroads extended their routes, they often encountered private property owners who were not inclined to sell their land. There were occasions known to many when a "farmer, moved by his affection for the land that was almost a part of himself, or instinctively fearful of the disruption which the railroad would bring to his familiar and beloved ways of life, or suspicious about the city strangers who would be brought to his door, or solicitous for the safety and peace of mind of his cattle and horses that would be terrified by the engine's noise and endangered by its speed, was flatly unwilling to sell at all."[10] In situations like these, the railroads asserted their rights of eminent domain and took over the land for modest compensation. The question of the meaning of the "public interest" was thus made concrete and symbolically real as law equated the interests of these vast corporations with the good of the public.

[10] Sullivan, *Our Times*, 194.

The railroad was reinforced as a negative symbol by a more contingent factor. Railroad executives could not help it if the map of a national system resembled an interlocking directorate, or if they needed to confiscate some land to complete a project. These sorts of images and activities are inherent to the building of railroads. Peculiarly American, however, was the practice of giving "passes" for unlimited free transportation each year to governors, party leaders, entire legislatures, municipal leaders, friendly newspaper editors, "to virtually every person in a position either to influence legislation, court decision, administrative action or public opinion." Party bosses could, and often did, solicit thousands of "trip passes" (good for only one trip) around election time.[11]

These passes not only symbolized the corruption that they induced; they also became signs of an American social hierarchy, as annual passes were treated as honors, flashed proudly as a "gesture of distinction." They might even be viewed as the precursors to "gold" and "platinum" credit cards in our time, except that the most prestigious annual passes were actually made of gold.[12]

The power of these negative symbols was made still more intense by their conflict with an often-repeated identity of the building of the railroad and the nation. Late-nineteenth-century presidents often spoke, in very general ways, of the railroad as exemplar and carrier of a beneficent national industrialism. The contrast between the railroad's promise and its real development as seen and felt alerted public attention and fueled public concern.

Railroad regulation raised fundamental regime-level questions. That fact alone distinguishes the case from the vast majority of legislation introduced in Congress. Closely connected to the character of the issue is its salience. Because the matters raised by railroad regulation were so fundamental, it is not surprising that considerable public attention was given to it. It need not have been so, however. Grave issues could, in some instances, remain shielded from public

[11] Ibid., 204.
[12] Ibid., 205, 210.

view or remain uninteresting to the public. In this case, public attention was riveted on the issue.

The high salience of railroad regulation was due in part to the power of symbols discussed above, but also to very extensive media coverage, which pitted colorful "muckrakers" against a well-endowed propaganda campaign engineered by the railroad industry. In 1905 especially, articles regularly appeared in most major magazines, including *McClure's*, *Arena*, and *Current Literature*. *McClure's* devoted several issues to detailed editorials by Ray Stannard Baker that were billed as "investigative reports" on the abuses of the railroads. Baker's particular gift was to explain the mechanics of railroad ratemaking and to connect that very technical discussion to questions regarding the quality of life on the farm or the birth and death of cities.[13]

Reinforcing and responding to public interest were congressmen who regularly appealed "to the people" on this issue. Robert La-Follette of Wisconsin made the issue the centerpiece of his calls for socialist reform. During the debate in the Senate, he made his maiden speech on this issue, speaking to a near-empty chamber until he declared: "I pause in my remarks to say this. I can not be wholly indifferent to the fact that Senators by their absence at this time indicate their want of interest in what I may have to say upon this subject. The public is interested. Unless this important question is rightly settled seats now temporarily vacant may be permanently vacated by those who have the right to occupy them at this time." David Chalmers reports that "the galleries applauded, and senators began to drift back into the chamber."[14]

The railroads did not remain mute while journalists "muckraked." Considerable sums were spent on a public relations campaign that spanned the continent. Ads were placed in newspapers; editorials and articles were commissioned; speeches of partisans

[13] See especially Ray Stannard Baker, "The Railroad Rate: A Study in Commercial Autocracy," *McClure's* 36 (November 1905).

[14] Chalmers, *Neither Socialism nor Monopoly*, 23. *Congressional Record*, 59th Cong. 1st Sess., 1906, vol. 40, p. 5688.

were published and circulated. And politicians were put on notice that their opinions were being monitored by the most powerful lobby in the nation. At the turn of the century, Americans could not avoid the issue.

Presidential Skills

In addition to the nature and salience of the issue, several political tactics contributed to Roosevelt's great success. These comprised a fairly sophisticated political strategy. Roosevelt coordinated his legislative and rhetorical efforts, bargained in a manner that appeared to give much but in fact gave little to his opponents, and articulated public principles with sufficient clarity to educate, not simply arouse public opinion.

Although Roosevelt was the first president to successfully appeal "over the heads" of Congress, he did so in a way that preserved, and did not preempt, Congress's deliberative capacities and responsibilities. Elmer Cornwell has pointed out that Roosevelt began and ended his "swings" before Congress took up the bill.[15] As Congress deliberated, the president eschewed public speech on the question, although he did encourage the speech of others, leak news items, and maintain private contact with congressmen. At one crucial juncture during the Senate debate in March, Roosevelt had his Bureau of Corporations release its report on the Standard Oil Corporation, showing that it had benefited by secret railroad rates. It was as if the "facts" could speak while Roosevelt himself remained statesmanlike.[16]

Roosevelt did not speak directly to the people on the eve of crucial votes, as is sometimes the case in our time, nor did he attack congressmen during the debate. For him, there was a marked contrast between campaign speeches, where such attacks were justified and a pleasure, and governing speech, where they were not. After passage of the legislation, Cornwell notes, Roosevelt took his case to the peo-

[15] Elmer Cornwell, *Presidential Leadership of Public Opinion* (Bloomington: Indiana University Press, 1965), 24–25.

[16] Pringle, *Roosevelt*, 421.

ple again, this time to facilitate its implementation by reassuring those who had lost that the law was not as radical as they had feared.[17] In this activity, Roosevelt abandoned nineteenth-century practice, to be sure, but he did so in a way that retained nineteenth-century objectives and accommodated that "nineteenth-century" institution, the Senate.

Roosevelt's principled posture might suggest a politician averse to compromise. To the extent that bargains undermined important principles, Roosevelt would not enter into them. And he did not offer his bargains in public address, though he might explain them as consistent with his principles after they were concluded. But Roosevelt was willing to trade support in ways that others believed were substantial compromises, but in fact were not.

John Morton Blum has persuasively shown that Roosevelt feigned interest in a bill to revise and reduce the tariff, in order to trade that project for support for his most important objective, railroad regulation. The Republican party was divided on the tariff issue. Roosevelt managed to consolidate the party by supporting the weaker side (for revision) until its political futility had been made manifest to its partisans. The president then agreed to support the opponents of tariff revision in exchange for support on railroad regulation.

In late November 1904, the president sent Speaker of the House Joe Cannon, "that archpriest of protection," a draft of a Special Message to Congress that urged tariff revision. Shortly thereafter, Roosevelt delivered his Annual Message, in which nothing was mentioned of the tariff, but which highlighted railroad regulation as "the most important legislative act now needed."[18]

Roosevelt turned his party's division on the tariff to his advantage, because it mirrored division on the railroad issue. "Stand-patters" on the tariff tended to be "laissez faire" regarding railroad regulation, while the advocates of tariff revision supported railroad regulation. "The low tariff, antirailroad group was to have one reform. The high tariff, prorailroad group to hold one redoubt. Saving what

[17] Cornwell, *Presidential Leadership*, 24–25.
[18] Blum, *The Republican Roosevelt*, 80.

he considered vital by sacrificing what he considered marginal, Roosevelt for the sake of railroad regulation jettisoned the draft of the Special Message on the tariff that had worried Cannon.'' Subsequently, Cannon—on record against regulation—provided no obstacle to the passage of the Hepburn Act. When others of Cannon's stripe tried to fight Hepburn, Roosevelt raised the tariff issue until they retreated. ''For eighteen months, he employed adroitly the specter of tariff agitation.''[19]

To make the distinction between matters of principle and matters of expediency required an understanding both of the place of a particular policy in the conspectus of administration efforts and of the core features of the particular policy itself. On the latter, I have already indicated how Roosevelt was willing to support various versions of judicial review. Each kind of compromise also required an ability to explain the shift in the president's position.

Roosevelt was an exceptionally skillful orator, well known for his engaging and distinctive speaking style. In addition, Roosevelt's speech was distinguished from most subsequent presidential speech by the care he took to state his case in terms of principle, not detailed policy; to repeat principles often; and to moderate public expectations of the success of the policy.

''As to the details of carrying out . . . general principles we cannot expect everybody to agree.''[20] Roosevelt left the details to Congress, where bargaining was, and ought to have been, public and legitimate. To articulate the principles clearly and often was the function of the presidential ''bully pulpit.'' Roosevelt used the issue of railroad regulation to raise and defend his principle of the ''square deal.''

> [At Dallas, Texas:] . . . no more intention of discrimination against the rich man than the poor man, or against the poor man than the rich

[19] Ibid., 85.
[20] Roosevelt, *The Roosevelt Policy*, 1:253 (Speech at Dallas, Texas, April 5, 1905). See also ibid., 1:263 (Speech at Denver, Colorado, May 9, 1905).

man; with the intention of safeguarding each man, rich or poor, poor or rich, in his rights, and giving him as nearly as may be a fair chance to do what his powers permit him to do.

[At Austin, Texas:] It is essential, in dealing thus by legislative action with corporate wealth, or indeed with wealth in any form, that we remember and act upon certain rules simple enough . . . to state, but not always easy to act upon. Most emphatically, we can not as good Americans bear hostility to any rich man as such any more than to any poor man as such. . . . That is my interpretation of the doctrine of the square deal.

[At Denver, Colorado:] A spirit of envy on the part of those less well off against the better off is as bad as and no worse than a spirit of arrogant disregard for the rights of the man of small means on the part of the man of large means. The arrogance and the envy are not two different qualities; they are the same quality shown by men under different circumstances.

[At Richmond, Virginia:] This government was formed with as its basic idea the principle of treating each man on his worth as a man, of paying no heed to whether he was rich or poor, no heed to his creed or his social standing, but only to the way in which he performed his duty to himself, to his neighbor, to the state. From this principle we can not afford to vary by so much as a hand's breadth.[21]

Roosevelt's principle was substantively moderate—mediating the claims of rich and poor. He made this moderation an even more general principle of statecraft. "We have been scrupulously careful on the one hand to be moderate in our promises, and on the other hand to keep these promises in letter and in spirit." If leaders overpromise, warned Roosevelt, "you will be laying up for yourselves a store of incalculable disappointment in the future." Because all campaigns for reform raise expectations of the populace, it is necessary for the leader to not only moderate his own promises and predictions, but also to combat the false hopes engendered by others. "I believe [the Hepburn Act] will work a measurable betterment for the public. Listen to what I say—a measurable benefit for the public. I do not believe that it will produce the millennium, or anything approaching it;

[21] Ibid., 1:253, 255, 261, 300. There are at least fifty more variations on, and amplifications of, this theme.

109

and I am quite certain that some of its most ardent advocates will be disappointed with the results.''[22]

THE OLD WAY REVISED

In his Inaugural Address of 1905, Roosevelt remarked, "Though the problems are new, though the tasks set before us differ from the tasks set before our fathers who founded and preserved this Republic, the spirit in which these tasks must be undertaken and these problems faced . . . remains essentially unchanged. . . .''[23]

Repeating this thought many times during his tenure as president, Roosevelt expressed a bi-level, Lincolnian approach to constitutional interpretation and statecraft. If the essential objects and most general principles of the Constitution could be adumbrated, specific constitutional prescriptions could be altered or abandoned as a matter of constitutional fidelity.

Roosevelt presumed that, periodically, the perspective of founder need be adopted to preserve or improve the constitutional order. Occasional "refoundings" would be necessary. In the same Inaugural, Roosevelt likens himself to Washington and Lincoln, founder and refounder. He suggests there, and often in subsequent addresses, that his is a time of fundamental crisis, in which the very capabilities of republican self-governance are to be tested. ". . . Upon the success of our experiment much depends, not only as regards our own welfare, but as regards the welfare of mankind. If we fail, the cause of free self-government throughout the world will rock to its foundations.''[24] This sentiment echoes the very first number of *The Federalist*:

[22] Ibid., 1:209 (also 254), 261, 278 (also 270).
[23] Roosevelt, ''Inaugural Address,'' March 4, 1905, in *The Roosevelt Policy*, 1:248; see also 1:265, 271–72.
[24] Roosevelt, *The Roosevelt Policy*, 248. In a remarkable speech devoted to the Hepburn Act, delivered in Denver, Colorado, Roosevelt again likens himself to Lincoln, a ''rescuer'' of the Republic (266).

> It has been frequently remarked that it seems to have been reserved to the people of this country, by their interest and example, to decide the important question, whether societies of men are really capable or not of establishing good government from reflection and choice, or whether they are forever destined to depend for their political constitutions on accident and force.[25]

As discussed in Chapter 2, *The Federalist* defended a theory of governance that would not require and did not provide support for the statesmanship of founders after the founding. Prominent among the arguments against popular leadership was the claim that an administrative republic would not need great leaders because the most difficult political issues would be replaced by the smaller concerns of citizens no longer contentious about the kind of regime they wished to constitute. The founders also feared provision for popular leadership because they expected that, as an institutional practice, statesmanship would quickly degenerate into demagoguery, which might raise anew the great divisions of class, section, or constitutive principle.

But what should the nation do if it found itself contending again with regime-level questions and disputes despite the founder's best efforts to settle those questions? And what should it do if those disputes were fueled by demagogues—demagogues who were not presidents, but demagogues nonetheless. This was the state of political life and these were the most important political questions in turn-of-the-century America, as Theodore Roosevelt viewed it. By speech and example, Roosevelt showed the need for plebiscitary leadership in order for the nation to achieve the founder's objectives, including those of moderating demagoguery and restoring the administrative republic.

Demagoguery had long been both an interest and a political concern for Roosevelt. During the presidential campaign of 1896, he accused William Jennings Bryan of demagoguery, and one of Roosevelt's campaign speeches was later republished with the title "The Menace of the Demagogue." The founder's worry to prevent

[25] *Federalist*, no. 1, p. 33.

"hard" demagogues—those who appeal to passion to exploit division—was Roosevelt's worry, too. "What [demagogues] appeal to is the spirit of social unrest, the spirit of discontent. They have invoked the aid of mean and somber vices of envy, of hatred for the well-to-do, and of sectional jealousy."[26]

Paradoxically, to oppose this form of leadership, Roosevelt adopted a rhetoric of alarm and exaggeration—that is, of untruth—in a political campaign. This sort of popular leadership could only be justified by its object or result, and could only be vouchsafed for the public by the character of its wielder. Said Roosevelt:

> Mssrs Bryan, Altgeld, Tillman, Debs, Coxey and the rest have not the power to rival the deeds of Marat, Barriere, and Robespierre, but they are strikingly like the leaders of the Terror of France in mental and moral attitudes, plus an added touch of the grotesque rising from the utter folly of trying to play such a rôle in such a country as ours. . . .
>
> [Altgeld] would connive at wholesale murder and would justify it by elaborate and cunning sophistry for reasons known only to this own tortuous soul.[27]

Roosevelt isolated two features of comtemporary demagoguery as the objects to which the central tenets of his public philosophy would be directed. Demagogues appealed to the passions of envy or of fear. Those who exaggerated the corruption of wealth appealed to the envy of the poor and middle class. Those who raised the specter of socialism appealed to the fears of the wealthy and middle class. From this observation, Roosevelt concluded that his public philosophy must distinguish individuals and corporations from the classes or categories in which they were subsumed. He would go after bad individuals and evil corporations, but he would chastize as demagogues those who opposed wealth as such or the impoverished as such.

He believed the nation was heading toward class war. "Above all, we need to remember that any kind of class animosity in the political world is, if possible, even more wicked, even more destructive to the

---

26 Theodore Roosevelt, "The Menace of the Demagogue," in *Works*, vol. 16 (New York: Charles Scribner's Sons, 1925), 401.
27 Roosevelt, "The Menace," 394–95.

national welfare, than sectional, race, or religious animosity.'' He wrote these startling words in a message to Congress in 1902. I pause to note that it is not necessary to assess the historical accuracy of Roosevelt's political analysis. Rather, we need only assume the plausibility of its central concerns. For if the nation could face a crisis of the sort he describes, then or later, the adequacy of the constitutional order to satisfy its original aspirations is seriously questioned.[28]

The campaign for the Hepburn Act was the forum in which Roosevelt publicly diagnosed and addressed his constitutional crisis. He tried to show how his seemingly novel policy and his new form of leadership were consistent with Hamiltonian principles even while they departed from nineteenth-century customs. Hamilton had argued in *The Federalist* against those who would attempt to guard against the abuses of governmental power by trimming power. Instead, argued Hamilton, government needed to possess all the power necessary to accomplish its ends.

> A government ought to contain in itself every power requisite to the full accomplishment of the objects committed to its care, and to the complete execution of the trusts for which it is responsible, free from every other control but a regard to the public good and to the sense of the people.[29]

To those who repeatedly warned of the potential for abuse of unlimited power, Hamilton responded: ''All observations founded upon the danger of usurpation ought to be referred to the composition and structure of the government, not to the extent or nature of its powers.''[30]

Roosevelt thought that opposition to railroad regulation posed the same issue, this time on two planes. The power to regulate the railroads was, like the power to tax, a necessary means toward legiti-

---

[28] Roosevelt, *The Roosevelt Policy*, 1:110. One indication that the debate raised fundamental issues, and also one measure of the distance between our political culture and Roosevelt's, is the fact that partisans of both sides of that debate used the terms ''capitalist'' and ''worker'' as a matter of course and without apology.

[29] *Federalist*, no. 31, p. 194.

[30] Ibid., 196.

mate ends; and the power to make this argument to the people was, likewise, a necessary power to accomplish legitimate purposes. Each power was subject to abuse, but the founders' argument for the legislative power to tax subverted their proscription of presidential power to speak. Said Roosevelt:

> The power of taxation is liable to grave abuse, and yet it must exist in the appropriate legislative body. You can not give any needed power to the representatives of the people without exposing yourselves to the danger of that power being abused. There must be the possibility of abuse or there can not be the possibility of effective use.[31]

Moreover, the power of popular speech is not necessary only to accomplish the positive purposes of government; it is necessary too, to accomplish the tasks of ''negative'' leadership emphasized by the founders. *The Federalist* candidly points out that it is the task of statesmen to act as a break upon public opinion, to contest it if it contradicts the Constitution or its own deeper aspirations. ''. . . It is the duty of the persons whom they have appointed to be the guardians of [the people's] interests to withstand the temporary delusion in order to give time and opportunity for more cool and sedate reflection.''[32] Roosevelt argued that popular leadership was sometimes necessary to withstand popular pressure. ''. . . If the public ignorantly demands that the railroad shall do more than it can with propriety do, then just as fearlessly [a leader] must antagonize public sentiment, even if the public sentiment is unanimous.''[33]

Pushed to its conclusion, the logic of Roosevelt's position justifies blatant appeals to passion, demagoguery in its worst guises, if that is necessary to preserve or restore the constitutional order. His attempt to exercise extraordinary power moderately, and with constant warnings about its possible abuse, was his attempt to resolve the perennial problem that faces any statesman or institutional theorist who wishes

[31] Roosevelt, *The Roosevelt Policy*, 1:264.
[32] *Federalist*, no. 71, p. 432.
[33] Roosevelt, *The Roosevelt Policy*, 1:254.

to provide for emergency power on the one hand, yet make it safe on the other.

Roosevelt's conception of statesmanship was the product of long reflection upon the difficulties of crisis rule. While governor of New York, he published his most thoughtful book, *Oliver Cromwell*, which probed the problem of providing order in the absence of a constitution. The key difficulty, thought Roosevelt, is to exercise necessary discretionary power without making that emergency power routine. "In great crises it may be necessary to overturn constitutions and disregard statutes, just as it might be necessary to establish a vigilance committee, or take refuge in a lynch law; but such a remedy is always dangerous, even when absolutely necessary; and the moment it becomes the habitual remedy it is proof that society is going backward."[34]

From Cromwell's errors Roosevelt learned the importance of forms and formalities in politics, and the need for the statesman to look to the long-term preservation of these forms even as he violates them in a crisis. "Cromwell himself was no theorist: in fact, he was altogether too little of one. He wished to do away with concrete acts of oppression and injustice, he sought to make life easier for any who suffered tangible wrong. Though earnestly bent upon doing justice . . . he failed to see that questions of form . . . might be themselves essential instead of, as they seemed to him, non-essential."[35] Roosevelt tried to temper the tendency of his theory to legitimize extreme behavior through the precedent of his example. He wished his moderate statesmanship, more than his immoderate theory, to be the precedent for future presidents.

His example did indeed become the precedent for future presi-

---

[34] Theodore Roosevelt, *Oliver Cromwell* (New York: Charles Scribner's Sons, 1923), 54. For the best statement of Roosevelt's and Woodrow Wilson's self-prescribed educations for statesmanship, see John Milton Cooper, *The Warrior and the Priest: Woodrow Wilson and Theodore Roosevelt* (Cambridge, Mass.: Harvard University Press, 1983).

[35] Roosevelt, *Cromwell*, 109.

dents, but not in the way Roosevelt had hoped. As I show in the next chapter, Woodrow Wilson constructed a still more radical constitutional theory than Roosevelt's, gaining support for it partly because of public familiarity with Roosevelt's popular leadership. By justifying Roosevelt's practice with a new theory that would make popular rhetoric routine, Wilson would transform the bully pulpit and Roosevelt's America.

· 5 ·

THE NEW WAY:
LEADERSHIP AS INTERPRETATION

Policy—where there is no absolute and arbitrary ruler to do the choosing
for a whole people—means massed opinion, and the forming of the mass
is the whole art and mastery of politics.[1]
   —Woodrow Wilson

The early years of the twentieth century were a period of ferment in
the presidency. The extensive use of popular rhetoric made in Teddy
Roosevelt's "swings around the circle" marked the beginning of a
new form of leadership. But Roosevelt had intended that his rhetoric
revive and perpetuate founding principles, and he justified his extraordinary behavior with "old" arguments. Inspirational rhetoric,
thought Roosevelt, was appropriate to crisis politics, to the reestab-
lishment of "normal" politics, and to the resuscitation of the *The
Federalist*'s understanding of the problems and prospects for democratic governance.

President Taft abandoned Roosevelt's popular practice, but began
one of his own. Remarkably for a renowned legal scholar and future

[1] Woodrow Wilson, "Leaderless Government," address before the Virginia Bar
Association, August 4, 1897, in *College and State*, ed. Ray Stannard Baker and
William E. Dodd, 2 vols. (New York: Harper & Brothers, 1925), 339.

chief justice of the Supreme Court, Taft abandoned constitutional argument completely in his messages to Congress. These messages also lacked the more rudimentary discipline of any sort of structured argument. Instead, Taft became the first president to regularly build his messages around "laundry lists" of legislative initiatives.

Woodrow Wilson settled modern practice for all presidents that were to follow him, uniting the inspirational form of Teddy Roosevelt with the policy specificity of Taft. More importantly, Wilson legitimized these practices by justifying his behavior with an ambitious reinterpretation of the constitutional order. In this chapter, I describe these new practices and this new constitutional understanding to show how Wilson transformed the presidency and American politics.

REINTERPRETING THE CONSTITUTIONAL PRINCIPLES: WOODROW WILSON'S STATECRAFT

Woodrow Wilson's comprehensive reinterpretation of the constitutional order appears, on first glance, to be internally inconsistent. Between the writing of his classic dissertation *Congressional Government* in 1884, and the publication of his well-known series of lectures, *Constitutional Government in the United States*, in 1908, Wilson shifted his position on important structural features of the constitutional system.

Early in his career Wilson depicted the House of Representatives as the potential motive force in American politics, and he urged reforms to make it more unified and energetic. He paid little attention to the presidency or the judiciary. In later years he focused his attention on the presidency. In his early writings Wilson urged a plethora of constitutional amendments that were designed to emulate the British parliamentary system, including proposals to synchronize the terms of representatives and senators with that of the president and to require presidents to choose leaders of the majority party as cabinet secretaries. Later Wilson abandoned formal amendment as a strategy, urging instead that the existing Constitution be reinterpreted to encompass his parliamentary views.

The last shift reveals that Wilson had also altered his views at a deeper theoretical level. Christopher Wolfe has shown that while the "early" Wilson held a traditional view of the Constitution as a document whose meaning persists over time, the "later" Wilson adopted an historicist understanding, claiming that the meaning of the Constitution changed as a reflection of the prevailing thought of successive generations.[2]

As interesting as these shifts in Wilson's thought are, they all rest upon an underlying critique of the American polity that he maintained consistently throughout his career. Wilson's altered constitutional proposals, indeed his altered understanding of constitutionalism itself, ought to be viewed as a series of strategic moves designed to remedy the same alleged systemic defects. Our task here is to review Wilson's understanding of those defects and to outline the doctrine he developed to contend with them—a doctrine whose centerpiece would ultimately be the rhetorical presidency.

Wilson's doctrine can be nicely counterpoised to the founders' understanding of demagoguery, representation, independence of the executive, and separation of powers. For clarity, these issues will be examined here in a slightly different order than before: separation of powers, representation, independence of the executive, and demagoguery.

Separation of Powers

For Wilson, separation of powers was the central defect of American politics. He was the first and most sophisticated proponent of the

---

[2] Woodrow Wilson, *Congressional Government: A Study in American Politics* (1884; reprint ed. Gloucester, Mass.: Peter Smith, 1973), preface to 15th printing, introduction; idem, *Constitutional Government in the United States* (New York: Columbia University Press, 1908); Christopher Wolfe, "Woodrow Wilson: Interpreting the Constitution," *Review of Politics* 41, no. 1 (January 1979): 131. See also Woodrow Wilson, "Cabinet Government in the United States," in Baker and Dodd, *College and State*, 1:19–42; Paul Eidelberg, *A Discourse on Statesmanship* (Urbana: University of Illinois Press, 1974), chs. 8 and 9; Harry Clor, "Woodrow Wilson," in *American Political Thought*, ed. Morton J. Frisch and Richard G. Stevens (New York: Charles Scribner's Sons, 1971); Robert Eden, *Political Leadership and Nihilism* (Gainesville: University of Florida Press, 1984), ch. 1.

now conventional argument that separation of powers is a synonym for "checks and balances," the negation of power by one branch over another. Yet Wilson's view was more sophisticated than its progeny because his ultimate indictment of the founders' conception was a functionalist one. Wilson claimed that under the auspices of the founders' view, formal and informal political institutions failed to promote true deliberation in the legislature and impeded energy in the executive.

Wilson characterized the founders' understanding as "Newtonian," a yearning for equipoise and balance in a machine-like system:

> The makers of our federal Constitution followed the scheme as they found it expounded in Montesquieu, followed it with genuine scientific enthusiasm. The admirable expositions of the *Federalist* read like thoughtful applications of Montesquieu to the political needs and circumstances of America. They are full of the theory of checks and balances. The President is balanced off against Congress, Congress against the President, and each against the courts. . . . Politics is turned into mechanics under [Montesquieu's] touch. The theory of gravitation is supreme.[3]

The accuracy of Wilson's portrayal of the founders may be questioned. He reasoned backward from the malfunctioning system as he found it to how they must have intended it. Wilson's depiction of the system rather than his interpretation of the founders' intentions is of present concern.

Rather than equipoise and balance, Wilson found a system dominated by Congress, with several attendant functional infirmities: major legislation frustrated by narrow-minded committees, lack of coordination and direction of policies, a general breakdown of deliberation, and an absence of leadership. Extra-Constitutional institutions—"boss"-led political parties chief among them—had sprung up to assume the functions not performed by Congress or the president, but they had not performed them well. Wilson also acknowledged that the formal institutions had not always performed

---

[3] Wilson, *Constitutional Government*, 56, 22; idem, "Leaderless Government," 337.

badly, that some prior Congresses (those of Webster and Clay) and some presidencies (those of Washington, Adams, Jefferson, Jackson, Lincoln, Roosevelt, and surprisingly, Madison) had been examples of forceful leadership.[4]

These two strands of thought—the growth of extra-constitutional institutions and the periodic excellence of the constitutional structures—led Wilson to conclude that the founders had mischaracterized their own system. The founders' rhetoric was "Newtonian," but their constitutional structure, like all government, was actually "Darwinian." Wilson explains:

> The trouble with the [Newtonian] theory is that government is not a machine but a living thing. It falls, not under the theory of the universe, but under the theory of organic life. It is accountable to Darwin, not to Newton. It is modified by its environment, necessitated by its tasks, shaped to its functions by the sheer pressure of life. No living thing can have its organs offset against each other as checks and live. On the contrary, its life is dependent upon their quick cooperation, their ready response to the commands of instinct or intelligence, their amicable community of purpose. Government is not a body of blind forces; it is a body of men, with highly differentiated functions, no doubt . . . but with a common task. . . . Their cooperation is indispensable. . . . This is not theory, but fact, and displays its force as fact, whatever may be thrown across its track. Living political constitutions must be Darwinian in structure and practice.[5]

The founders' doctrine had affected the working of the structure to the extent that the power of the political branches was interpreted mechanically and many of the structural features reflected the Newtonian yearning. A tension arose between the "organic" core of the system and the politicians' and citizens' "mechanical" understanding of it. Thus, "the constitutional structure of the government has hampered and limited [the president's] actions but it has not prevented [them]." Wilson tried to resolve the tension between the understanding of American politics as Newtonian and its actual Darwinian char-

---

[4] Wilson, *Congressional Government*, 141, 149, 164, 195.
[5] Wilson, *Constitutional Government*, 56.

acter to make the evolution self-conscious and thereby more rational and effective.[6]

Wilson attacked the founders for relying on mere "parchment barriers" to effectuate a separation of powers. This claim is an obvious distortion of founding views. In *The Federalist*, nos. 47 and 48, the argument is precisely that the federal constitution, unlike earlier state constitutions, would *not* rely primarily upon parchment distinctions of power but upon differentiation of institutional structures.[7] However, Wilson's discussion of parchment barriers reveals an important difference between his and the founders' view of the same problem. Both worried over the tendency of legislatures to dominate in republican systems.

To mitigate the danger posed by legislatures, the founders had relied primarily upon an independent president with an office structured to give its occupant the personal incentive and means to stand up to Congress when it exceeded its authority. These structural features included a nonlegislative mode of election, constitutionally fixed salary, qualified veto, four-year term, and indefinite reeligibility. Although the parchment powers of Congress and the president overlapped (contrary to Wilson's depiction of them), the demarcation of powers proper to each branch would result primarily from political interplay and conflict between the political branches rather than from a theoretical drawing of lines by the judiciary.[8]

Wilson offered a quite different view. First, he claimed that because of the inadequacy of mere parchment barriers, Congress, in the latter half of the nineteenth century, had encroached uncontested

---

[6] Ibid., 60; see also Wilson, *Congressional Government*, 28, 30, 31, 187.

[7] *Federalist*, nos. 47 and 48, 300–313. Consider Madison's statement in *Federalist*, no. 48, 308–309: "Will it be sufficient to mark with precision, the boundaries of these departments in the Constitution of the government, and to trust to these parchment barriers against the encroaching spirit of power? This is the security which appears to have been principally relied upon by the compilers of most of the American Constitutions. But experience assures us that the efficacy of the provision has been greatly overrated; and that some more adequate defense is indispensably necessary for the more feeble against the more powerful members of the government. The legislative department is everywhere extending the sphere of its activity and drawing all power into its impetuous vortex."

[8] Schmitt, "Executive Privilege."

upon the executive sphere. Second, he contended that when the president's institutional check was employed, it took the form of a ''negative''—prevention of a bad outcome rather than provision for a good one. In this view, separation of powers hindered efficient, co-ordinated, well-led policy.

[The president] may, no doubt, stand in the way of measures with a veto very hard to overleap; and we think oftentimes with deep comfort of the laws he can kill when we are afraid of the majority in Congress. Congressional majorities are doubtless swayed, too, by what they know the President will do with the bills they send him. But they are swayed sometimes one way and sometimes the other, according to the temper of the times and state of parties. They as often make his assured veto a pretext for recklessness as a reason for self-restraint. They take a sort of irresponsible and defiant pleasure in ''giving him the dare.'' . . . It is a game in which he has no means of attack and few effective weapons of defense.[9]

Wilson did not wish to bolster structures to thwart the legislature. He preferred that the president and Congress be fully integrated into, and implicated in, each others' activities. Rather than merely assail Congress, Wilson would tame, or as it were, domesticate it. Separation would be replaced by institutionally structured cooperation. Cooperation was especially necessary because the president lacked the energy he needed, energy that could be provided only by policy backed by Congress and its majority. Although Congress had failed as a deliberative body, it could now be restored to its true function by presidential leadership that raised and defended key policies.

These latter two claims actually represent the major purposes of the Wilsonian theory: leadership and deliberation. Unlike the founders, who saw these two functions in conflict, Wilson regarded them as dependent upon each other. In ''Leaderless Government'' he stated:

I take it for granted that when one is speaking of a representative legislature he means by an ''efficient organization'' an organization which provides for deliberate, and deliberative, action and which enables the nation to affix responsibility for what is done and not done.

[9] Wilson, ''Leaderless Government,'' 340, 357; idem, *Congressional Government*, 158, 201; idem, ''Cabinet Government,'' 24–25.

The Senate is deliberate enough; but it is hardly deliberative after its ancient and better manner. . . . The House of Representatives is neither deliberate nor deliberative. We have not forgotten that one of the most energetic of its recent Speakers thanked God, in his frankness, that the House was not a deliberative body. It has not the time for the leadership of argument. . . . For debate and leadership of that sort the House must have a party organization and discipline such as it has never had.[10]

At this point, it appears that the founders and Wilson differed on the means to common ends. Both wanted "deliberation" and an "energetic" executive, but each proposed different constitutional arrangements to secure those objectives. In fact, their differences went much deeper, for each theory defined deliberation and energy to mean different things. These differences, hinted at in the above quotation, will become clearer as we examine Wilson's reinterpretations of representation and of independence of the executive.

Representation

In the discussion of the founding perspective, the competing requirements of popular consent and insulation from public opinion as a requisite of impartial judgment were canvassed. Woodrow Wilson gave much greater weight to the role of public opinion as the ordinary conduct of representative government than did the founders. Some scholars have suggested that Wilson's rhetoric and the institutional practices he established (especially regarding the nomination of presidential candidates) are the major sources of contemporary efforts toward a more "participatory" democracy. However, Wilson's understanding of representation, like his view on separation of powers, is more sophisticated than his followers'.[11]

[10] Wilson, "Leaderless Government," 346; at the time he wrote this, Wilson was thinking of leadership internal to the House, but he later came to see the president performing this same role. Wilson, *Constitutional Government*, 69–77; see also idem, *Congressional Government*, 76, 97–98.

[11] Eidelberg, *Discourse*, chs. 8 and 9; James W. Ceaser, *Presidential Selection: Theory and Development* (Princeton, N.J.: Princeton University Press, 1979), ch. 4, conclusion.

Wilson categorically rejected the Burkean view of the legislator who is elected for his quality of judgment and position on a few issues and then left free to exercise that judgment:

> It used to be thought that legislation was an affair to be conducted by the few who were instructed for the benefit of the many who were uninstructed: that statesmanship was a function of origination for which only trained and instructed men were fit. Those who actually conducted legislation and undertook affairs were rather whimsically chosen by Fortune to illustrate this theory, but such was the ruling thought in politics. The Sovereignty of the People, however, that great modern principle of politics, has created a different conception—or, if so be it, in the slowness of our thought we hang on to the old conception, has created a very different practice. When we are angry with public men nowadays we charge them with subserving instead of forming and directing public opinion . . . [but] we [now] know the principle that public opinion must be truckled to (if you will use a disagreeable word) in the conduct of government. . . . And it is a dignified proposition with us—is it not?—that as is the majority, so ought the government to be.[12]

Wilson did not think that his view was equivalent to "direct democracy" or to subservience to public opinion (understood, as it often is today, as response to public opinion polls). He favored an interplay between representative and constituent that would, in fact, educate the constituent. This process differed, at least in theory, from the older attempts to "form" public opinion: it did not begin in the minds of the elite but in the hearts of the mass. Wilson called the process of fathoming the people's desires (often only vaguely known to the people until instructed) "interpretation." Interpretation was the core of leadership for him.[13] Before exploring its meaning further, it will be useful to dwell upon Wilson's notion of the desired interplay between the "leader-interpreter" and the people so that we

---

[12] Woodrow Wilson, *Leaders of Men*, ed. T. H. Vail Motter (Princeton: N.J.: Princeton University Press, 1952), 39. This is the manuscript of an oft-repeated lecture that Wilson delivered in the 1890s. See also idem, *Congressional Government*, 195, 214.

[13] Wilson, *Leaders of Men*, 39; idem, *Constitutional Government*, 49. See also idem, *Congressional Government*, 78, 136–37.

may see how Wilson's understanding of deliberation differed from the founders'.

For the founders, deliberation simply meant reasoning on the merits of policy. The character and content of deliberation thus would vary with the character of the policy at issue. In "normal" times, there would be extensive squabbles by competing interests. Deliberation would occur to the extent that such interests were compelled to offer a response to arguments made by the others. The arguments might be relatively crude, specialized, and technical, or they might involve matters of legal or constitutional propriety. But in none of these instances would they resemble the great debates over fundamental principles—for example, over the question whether to promote interests in the first place. Great questions were the stuff of crisis politics, and the founders placed much hope in securing the distinction between crisis and normal political life.

Wilson effaced the distinction between "crisis" and "normal" political argument.

> Crises give birth and a new growth to statesmanship because they are peculiarly periods of action . . . [and] also of unusual opportunity for gaining leadership and a controlling and guiding influence. . . . And we thus come upon the principle . . . that governmental forms will call to the work of administration able minds and strong hearts constantly or infrequently, according as they do or do not afford them *at all times* an opportunity of gaining and retaining a commanding authority and an undisputed leadership in the nation's councils.[14]

Woodrow Wilson's lament that little deliberation took place in Congress was not that the merits of policies were left unexplored, but rather that because the discussions were not elevated to the level of major contests of principle, the public generally did not interest itself. True deliberation, he urged, would rivet the attention of press and public, while what substituted for it in his day were virtually secret contests of interest-based factions. Wilson rested this view on three observations. First, the congressional workload was parceled

---

[14] Wilson, "Cabinet Government," 34–35. See also idem, "Leaderless Government," 354; idem, *Congressional Government*, 72, 136–37.

among specialized standing committees, whose decisions usually were ratified by the respective houses without any general debate. Second, the arguments that did take place in committee were technical and structured by the "special pleadings" of interest groups, whose advocates adopted the model of legal litigation as their mode of discussion. As Wilson characterized committee debates:

> They have about them none of the searching, critical, illuminating character of the higher order of parliamentary debate, in which men are pitted against each other as equals, and urged to sharp contest and masterful strife by the inspiration of political principle and personal ambition, through the rivalry of parties and the competition of policies. They represent a joust between antagonistic interests, not a contest of principles.[15]

Finally, because debates were hidden away in committee, technical, and interest-based, the public cared little about them. "The ordinary citizen cannot be induced to pay much heed to the details, or even the main principles of lawmaking," Wilson wrote, "unless something else more interesting than the law itself be involved in the pending decision of the lawmakers."[16] For the founders this would not have been disturbing, but for Wilson the very heart of representative government was the principle of publicity: "The informing function of Congress should be preferred even to its legislative function."[17] The informing function was to be preferred both as an end in itself and because the accountability of public officials required policies that were connected with one another and explained to the people. Argument from "principle" would connect policy and present constellations of policies as coherent wholes to be approved or disapproved by the people. "Principles, as statesmen conceive them, are threads to the labyrinth of circumstances."[18]

Wilson attacked separation of powers in an effort to improve lead-

[15] Wilson, *Congressional Government*, 69, 72.

[16] Ibid., 82.

[17] Ibid., 198.

[18] Wilson, *Leaders of Men*, 46. See also idem, "Cabinet Government," 20, 28–32.

ership for the purpose of fostering deliberation. "Congress cannot, under our present system . . . be effective for the instruction of public opinion, or the cleansing of political action." As mentioned at the outset of this chapter, Wilson first looked to Congress itself, specifically to its speaker, for such leadership. Several years after the publication of *Congressional Government*, Wilson turned his attention to the president. "There is no trouble now about getting the president's speeches printed and read, every word," he wrote at the turn of the century.[19]

Independence of the Executive

The attempt to bring the president into more intimate contact with Congress and the people raises the question of the president's "independence." Wilson altered the meaning of this notion, which originally had been that the president's special authority came independently from a Constitution, not from Congress or the people. The president's station thus afforded him the possibility and responsibility of taking a perspective on policy different from either Congress or the people. Wilson urged us to consider the president as receiving his authority independently through a mandate from the people. For Wilson, the president remained "special," but now because he was the only governmental officer with a national mandate.[20]

Political scientists today have difficulty in finding mandates in election years, let alone between them, because of the great number of issues and the lack of public consensus on them. Wilson understood this problem and urged the leaders to sift through the multifarious currents of opinion to find a core of issues that he believed reflected majority will even if the majority was not fully aware of it. The leader's rhetoric could translate the people's felt desires into public policy. Wilson cited Daniel Webster as an example of such an interpreter of the public will:

[19] Wilson, *Congressional Government*, 76; ibid., Preface to 15th printing, 22–23.
[20] Ibid., 187.

128

The nation lay as it were unconscious of its unity and purpose, and he called it into full consciousness. It could never again be anything less than what he had said it was. It is at such moments and in the mouths of such interpreters that nations spring from age to age in their development.[21]

"Interpretation" involves two skills. First, the leader must understand the true majority sentiment underneath the contradictory positions of factions and the discordant views of the mass. Second, the leader must explain the people's true desires to them in a way that is easily comprehended and convincing.

Wilson's desire to raise politics to the level of rational disputation and his professed aim to have leaders educate the mass are contradictory. Candidly, he acknowledges that the power to command would require simplification of the arguments to accommodate the mass: "The arguments which induce popular action must always be broad and obvious arguments; only a very gross substance of concrete conception can make any impression on the minds of the masses."[22] Not only is argument simplified, but disseminating "information," a common concern of contemporary democratic theory, is not the function of a deliberative leader in Wilson's view:

> Men are not led by being told what they don't know. Persuasion is a force, but not information; and persuasion is accomplished by creeping into the confidence of those you would lead. Their confidence is gained by arguments which they can assimilate: by the things which find easy entrance into their minds and are easily transmitted to the palms of their hands or the ends of their walking sticks in the shape of applause. . . . Mark the simplicity and directness of the arguments and ideas of [true leaders.] The motives which they urge are elemental; the morality

[21] Wilson, *Constitutional Government*, 49. Today, the idea of a mandate as objective assessment of the will of the people has been fused with the idea of leader as interpreter. Presidents regularly appeal to the results of elections as legitimizing those policies that they believe ought to reflect majority opinion. On the "false" claims to represent popular will, see Stanley Kelley Jr., *Interpreting Elections* (Princeton, N.J.: Princeton University Press, 1984).

[22] Wilson, *Leaders of Men*, 20, 26. "[The masses] must get their ideas very absolutely put, and [they] are much readier to receive a half-truth which they can understand than a whole truth which has too many sides to be seen at once."

which they seek to enforce is large and obvious; the policy they emphasize, purged of all subtlety.[23]

Demagoguery

Wilson's understanding of leadership raises again the problem of demagoguery. What distinguishes a leader-interpreter from a demagogue? Who is to make this distinction? The founders feared that there was no institutionally effective way to exclude the demagogue if popular oratory during "normal" times was encouraged. Indeed, the term "leader," which appears a dozen times in *The Federalist*, is used disparagingly in all but one instance, and that one is a reference to leaders of the Revolution.[24]

Wilson was sensitive to this problem. "The most despotic of governments under the control of wise statesmen is preferable to the freest ruled by demagogues," he wrote. Wilson relied upon two criteria to distinguish the demagogue from the leader, one based upon the nature of the appeal, the other upon the character of the leader. The demagogue appeals to "the momentary and whimsical popular mood, the transitory or popular passion," whereas the leader appeals to "true" and durable majority sentiment. The demagogue is motivated by the desire to augment personal power, whereas the leader is more interested in fostering the permanent interests of the community. "The one [trims] to the inclinations of the moment, the other [is] obedient to the permanent purposes of the public mind."[25]

Theoretically, there are a number of difficulties with these distinctions. If popular opinion is the source of the leader's rhetoric, what basis apart from popular opinion itself is there to distinguish the "permanent" from the "transient"? If popular opinion is constantly evolving, what sense is there to the notion of "the permanent purposes of the public mind"? Yet the most serious difficulties are prac-

[23] Ibid., 29.

[24] I am indebted to Robert Eden for the point about *The Federalist*. See also Ceaser, *Presidential Selection*, 192–97.

[25] Wilson, "Cabinet Government," 37; idem, *Leaders of Men*, 45–46.

tical ones. Assuming it is theoretically possible to distinguish the leader from the demagogue, how is that distinction to be incorporated into the daily operation of political institutions? Wilson offered a threefold response to this query.

First, he claimed that his doctrine contained an ethic that could be passed on to future leaders. Wilson hoped that politicians' altered understanding of what constituted success and fame could provide some security. He constantly pointed to British parliamentary practice, urging that long training in debate had produced generations of leaders and few demagogues. Wilson had taught at Johns Hopkins, Bryn Mawr, Wesleyan, and Princeton, and at each of those institutions he had established debating societies modeled on the Oxford Union.[26]

Second, Wilson placed some reliance upon the public's ability to judge character:

> Men may be clever and engaging speakers, such as are to be found, doubtless, at half the bars of the country, without being equipped even tolerably for any of the high duties of the statesman; but men can scarcely be orators without the force of character, that readiness of resource, that clearness of vision, that grasp of intellect, that courage of conviction, that earnestness of purpose and that instinct and capacity for leadership which are the eight horses that draw the triumphal chariot of every leader and ruler of free men. We could not object to being ruled by such men.[27]

According to Wilson, the public need not appeal to a complex standard or theory to distinguish demagoguery from leadership, but could easily recognize "courage," "intelligence," and "correctness of purpose"—signs that the leader is not a demagogue. Wilson does not tell us why prior publics *have* fallen prey to enterprising demagogues, but the major difficulty with this second source of restraint is that public understanding of the leader's character would come from his oratory rather than from a history of his political activity or

---

[26] See, for example, Wilson, *Congressional Government*, 143–47.
[27] Ibid., 144.

from direct contact with him. The public's understanding of character might be based solely on words.

Finally, Wilson suggests that the natural conservatism of public opinion, its resistance to innovation that is not consonant with the speed and direction of its own movement, will afford still more safety:

> Practical leadership may not beckon to the slow masses of men from beyond some dim, unexplored space or some intervening chasm: it must daily feel the road to the goal proposed, knowing that it is a slow, very slow, evolution to the wings, and that for the present, and for a very long future also, Society must walk, dependent upon practicable paths, incapable of scaling sudden heights. . . .[28]

These assurances of security against demagogues are all unsatisfactory. They do not adequately distinguish the polity in which Wilson worked from others in which demagogues have prevailed, including some southern states in this country. However, his arguments should be considered as much for the theoretical direction and emphases that they imply as for the particular weaknesses they reveal. Wilson's doctrine stands on the premise that the need for more energy in the political system is greater than the risk incurred through the possibility of demagoguery.[29] This represents a major shift, indeed a reversal, of the founding perspective. If Wilson's argument regarding demagoguery was strained or inadequate, it was a price he was willing to pay to remedy what he regarded as the founders' inadequate provision for an energetic executive.

New Standards, New Forms

The development of the practices of presidential rhetoric in the twentieth century reflects the force of Woodrow Wilson's constitutional reasoning and amplifies its meaning. Wilson wrote and spoke about speaking often enough to articulate and justify new standards and

[28] Wilson, *Leaders of Men*, 45.
[29] Wilson, *Congressional Government*, 144.

new forms of address embodying his larger views of leadership. Wilson altered the two principle nineteenth-century prescriptions for presidential speech.

First, policy rhetoric, which had formerly been *written* and addressed principally to *Congress*, would now be *spoken* and addressed principally to the *people* at large. Of course, special messages, proclamations, executive orders, and other documents would continue their nineteenth-century forms (at least with respect to being written), but their importance in the conspectus of executive communications would greatly diminish. Truly important speeches would be delivered orally, where the visible and audible performance would become as important as the prepared text. For example, Wilson revived the practice (abandoned by Jefferson) of appearing in person before Congress to deliver the State of the Union Address. Although it was spoken in Congress (and was therefore more constrained than the speech would be if given in the open air to the people at large), Wilson made it clear in his first Address that his principal audience was the people at large, that he would approach Congress through the people. For this reason, he did not revive the whole pre-Jeffersonian practice; he saw no need for a "reply" to the Address from Congress or for the interbranch deliberation that would attend a president's reply to the reply.[30]

Wilson self-consciously changed nearly 150 years of practice because he thought that the Constitution's provisions, though arguably intended to promote leadership through rhetoric, had not in fact enhanced energy in the executive.

> Of course [the president] can send a message to Congress whenever he likes—the Constitution bids him do so "from time to time," in order to "give the Congress information of the state of the union and recommend to their consideration such measures as he shall deem necessary and expedient"; and we know that if he be a man of real power and statesmanlike initiative he may often hit the wish and purpose of the nation so in the quick in what he urges upon Congress that the House will heed him promptly and seriously enough. But there is a

[30] Ibid., 161.

stubborn and very natural pride in the House with respect to this matter. . . . It is easy to stir their resentment by too much suggestion. . . . In all ordinary times the President . . . preserves a sort of modesty, a tone as if chronicler merely, and setter forth of things administrative, when he addresses Congress. He makes it his study to use only a private influence and never seem a maker of resolutions. And even when the occasion is extraordinary and his own mind made up, he argues and urges—he cannot command.[31]

Wilson goes on in this text to contrast the modern president's powerlessness with the forceful leadership of Washington, Adams, Jefferson, Monroe, and Jackson. Since those presidents did follow nineteenth-century rhetorical prescriptions, the crucial factor accounting for their success, thought Wilson, was their "stature and eminence." While Wilson's argument is ambiguous on this point, it appears that he either understood eminence as popularity or, more probably, believed that a doctrinally prescribed routine appeal to the people was a good substitute for "reputation" (the founders' preferred term). Just as early leaders drew upon their reputations to lead Congress, so could modern leaders draw upon public opinion.

In addition to the argument for executive energy, Wilson made his case for speech on grounds of accountability.

Correspondence between [president and Congress] is carried on by means of written communications, which, like all formal writings, are vague, or by means of private examinations of officials in committee rooms to which the whole House cannot be audience. No one who has read official documents needs to be told how easy it is to conceal the essential truth under the apparently candid and all-disclosing phrases of a voluminous and particularizing report; how different those answers are which are given with the pen from a private office from those with the tongue when the Speaker is looking an assembly in the face.[32]

The second kind of standard that governed nineteenth-century practice affected the form of argument of those speeches that were given. Nineteenth-century speeches were often constrained by a con-

[31] Wilson, "Leaderless Government," 341. See also Richard Neustadt, *Presidential Power*, 3rd ed. (New York: John Wiley & Sons, 1980), 23–25.

[32] Wilson, *Congressional Government*, 109.

stitutional tradition of argument and by other customs consistent with the general doctrine. One could say that the tone and character of popular speeches was set, or at least strongly influenced, by that of written messages to Congress. After Wilson, a reverse trend prevailed: the character of important messages to Congress would be shaped by the development of standards for popular speech.

Wilson sought to establish two ideal types of popular address. First, he pressed for more "visionary" speech, which would articulate a picture of the future and impel a populace toward it. Rather than appealing to, and reinvigorating established principles, this forward-looking speech taps the public's feelings and articulates its wishes. At its best it creates, rather than explains, principles.

> A nation is led by a man who . . . speaks, not the rumors of the street, but a new principle for a new age; a man in whose ears the voices of the nation do not sound like the accidental and discordant notes that come from the voice of a mob, but concurrent and concordant like the united voices of a chorus, whose many meanings, spoken by melodious tongues, unite in his understanding in a single meaning and reveal to him a single vision, so that he can speak what no man else knows, the common meaning of the common voice.[33]

In his first inaugural, Wilson tried to craft just this sort of visionary speech. This address is remarkable because we are not left to infer that visionary speech was intended. Wilson tells us so in the speech.

> At last a vision has been vouchsafed us of our life as a whole. We see the bad with the good, the debased and decadent with the sound and vital. With this vision we approach new affairs. . . .
>
> This is the high enterprise of the new day; To lift everything that concerns our life as a nation to the light that shines from the hearthfire of every man's conscience and vision of the right. . . .
>
> We know our task to be no mere task of politics but a task which shall search us through and through, whether we be able to understand our time and the need of our people, whether we be indeed their

---

[33] Woodrow Wilson, "Abraham Lincoln: A Man of the People," in Baker and Dodd, ed., *College and State*, 2:94–95. See also idem, "A Memorandum on Leadership, May 5, 1902," in *The Papers of Woodrow Wilson*, ed. Arthur S. Link (Princeton, N.J.: Princeton University Press, 1966–), 12:365.

spokesmen and interpreters, whether we have the pure heart to comprehend and the rectified will to choose our high course of action.[34]

Inspirational speech is often moral, even moralistic, as well. Later Franklin Roosevelt was to call the president the nation's only "moral trumpet," and he would be credited by many scholars with founding the "modern" presidency; but the practice began with Theodore Roosevelt, and the legitimating doctrine was uttered by Wilson.

The second sort of speech Wilson encouraged was what I label the "policy-stand" speech. This sort of rhetoric aims at specificity. It need not convey much information (and Wilson believed not much could be conveyed), but it should indicate where the president stood or what he would do regarding the issues of the day. Wilson often referred to these stands as "definite policies," and his insistence upon them grew out of his concern for greater accountability. Wilson did not question the compatibility of his inspirational principle-creating speech with the policy-stand type. "And with leaders whose leadership was earned in an open war of principle against principle, by the triumph of one opinion over all opposing opinions, parties must from the necessities of the case have definite policies."[35]

Yet it is difficult in practice for a single speech to be inspirational and highly specific at the same time. Consider, for example, President Carter's "moral malaise" speech. Beginning with an analysis that pointed to a deep sickness in the American soul, it ends with a call to conserve energy and tax oil companies. Perhaps to avoid this sort of difficulty, Wilson generally did not mix his modes of address. (A partial exception to this generalization is his League of Nations campaign, discussed here in the next chapter.) Wilson's problem and his adopted solution are still with us. Recall that President Carter's first two State of the Union messages attempted, with predictable difficulty, to be both inspirational and exhaustive as to specific legislative initiatives. In his third year, however, he adopted the practice of

[34] Wilson, *Papers*, 27:150.
[35] Wilson, "Cabinet Government," 36–37; see also idem, "Leaderless Government," 355.

sending two State of the Union messages, a short televised inspirational effort, and a voluminous "laundry list" the following day.

COMPARING RHETORIC: OLD AND NEW

If the practices Wilson established took hold and replaced those of the nineteenth century, change should be evident when the bodies of "official" rhetoric for each century are compared. A comparative "content analysis" as large as this is difficult for two reasons. First, we have an official record of the entire nineteenth-century corpus of presidential messages and papers, commissioned by Congress and compiled by James D. Richardson. However, Congress only commissioned such a record for recent twentieth-century Presidents (Truman to the present, and Hoover). The rationale for Congress's decision was that it would avoid unnecessary expense, since adequate private compilations are available for some of the other twentieth-century presidents. These private compilations, however, were constructed on such varied principles of organization and inclusion that they were inadequate for our purposes. To ensure a comparison of "official" rhetoric, our major source for the twentieth century is the set of public papers extending from Truman through the third year of Carter's term.

Second, the sheer number of communications (approximately twenty-five thousand) precluded reading them all, especially since intelligent judgment of the effect of doctrinal change requires that one treat the whole document, rather than words, sentences, or paragraphs, as the unit of analysis. Because careful consideration of the audience, form, and content of whole speeches and messages requires considerable time, a random sample of documents from each century was selected. Yet because the primary sample could produce few examples of two important categories of rhetoric, inaugural addresses and State of the Union messages, I supplemented it with another, composed of all inaugural and State of the Union messages in both centuries. Although manageable, this stratified sample still pro-

TABLE 5.1 Principal Presidential Audiences in the Nineteenth
and Twentieth Centuries
(Percent and Number of Speeches Sampled)

Audience	Nineteenth Century		Twentieth Century	
	%	(N)	%	(N)
People	7	(23)	41	(138)
Congress	85	(272)	21	(71)
Bureaucracy	6	(20)	6	(20)
Individuals	1	(4)	21	(70)
Interest Groups	0	(0)	2	(6)
Foreign Nations	0	(0)	9	(31)
Total	100	(319)	100	(336)

duced a considerable number of documents to be read and coded—
just over 900.[36]

If Wilson's doctrine had taken hold and accomplished its objectives, we would expect at least three broad twentieth-century
changes: (1) Less rhetoric would be addressed principally to Congress and more to the people at large; (2) more emphasis would be
placed upon oral speeches and less upon written messages; and (3)
the above two changes would bring with them a change in structure
of argument, with the twentieth-century sample manifesting structures more appropriate to "inspirational" and "policy-stand" rhetoric. With minor qualifications, the data presented below substanti-
ate each of these expectations.

Documents were classified according to their principal addressee.
As Table 5.1 indicates, there are obvious differences between the
centuries. Only 7 percent of official rhetoric (mainly proclamations)
is addressed principally to the people in the nineteenth century, as

[36] The material was coded by a group consisting of three graduate students and
me, employing standard content analysis practices. We examined twenty-five variables, although only a few are discussed here. Intercoder reliability was very high—
indeed, near-perfect agreement on all coding judgments reported here.

against 41 percent in the twentieth century. Confirming one of the claims made in Chapter 2 on the basis of the historical survey, most nineteenth-century rhetoric (85 percent) was principally aimed toward Congress.[37] Twentieth-century doctrine has brought with it a greater variety of types of presidential rhetoric and a reallocation of emphasis placed upon the traditional types. Classification according to type required little interpretive intrusion since nearly all of the rhetoric was officially labeled.

As indicated in Table 5.2, the most noticeable twentieth-century development is the use of oral speech. Virtually all nineteenth-century communication was written. There were some nineteenth-century speeches (i.e., inaugural addresses and some Messages to Congress), but these were so few (less than 1 percent) that they were not picked up by our sample. By contrast, 42 percent of presidential rhetoric today is spoken. Not only do we have presidential "speech" today, whereas there was virtually none, officially, in the previous century, but also speech today constitutes much of presidential communication altogether. Written communications to Congress have dwindled to 19 percent of the president's total persuasive effort. The practice of issuing "statements" was not done officially in the nineteenth century.[38]

[37] Of course, most documents have, and are intended to have, several audiences. The principal audience could often be gleaned from the text, but coders were cautioned not to assume that a certain style "went with" a particular audience in the absence of specific indications in the text. In many instances the principal audience is noted at the head of the text (e.g., "To the Congress of the United States," or "My Fellow Americans"). Broadcast addresses were automatically coded "people," except those which were speeches delivered in foreign nations, which were automatically coded "foreign nation." Documents addressed to individuals or small sets of individuals and not indicating an intention of wider circulation at the time they were first communicated were coded "individual," while those circulated were occasionally coded "people" or "bureaucracy."

[38] Actually, more statements than are estimated here have been issued by twentieth-century presidents. Until Carter, a record was kept of such statements (which includes "press releases") in the form of a list appended to the *Public Papers*. Only those deemed significant or "typical" were printed in full, even though all had been issued officially. (Our summary does not take into account those lists, although this does not alter the thrust of our discussion.) With Carter, *all* statements are included in the Weekly Compilation of Presidential Documents.

TABLE 5.2 Types of Presidential Speech in the Nineteenth
and Twentieth Centuries
(Percent and Number of Speeches Sampled)

Type	Nineteenth Century		Twentieth Century	
	%	(N)	%	(N)
Speeches (all oral)	0	(0)	42	(141)
Informal remarks	0	(0)	11	(37)
Press conferences	0	(0)	8	(26)
Proclamations	9	(30)	2	(6)
Executive orders	7	(21)	2	(5)
Messages to Congress (all)	82	(259)	19	(63)
Annual	2	(4)	0	(0)
Special	72	(228)	16	(53)
Reports	0	(0)	1	(3)
Veto	9	(27)	2	(7)
Bill signings	1	(3)	8	(26)
Appointments and nominations	1	(3)	6	(20)
Memoranda and letters	1	(3)	7	(25)
Individual	1	(2)	5	(18)
Executive branch	0	(1)	2	(7)
Statements				
Joint (with foreign				
governments)	0	(0)	1	(4)
Policy	0	(0)	7	(22)
Nonpolicy	0	(0)	2	(7)
Commemorative	0	(0)	2	(8)
Citations	0	(0)	2	(8)
Total	100	(319)	100	(336)

Table 5.2 makes clear that twentieth-century presidents have more acknowledged tools to influence public opinion and to make public policy. But it also suggests that they operate in a context in which it is more likely that policy might be made despite their wishes. Everything a president publicly says and much of what is written by him or

his subordinates is "official," and therefore "policy." Paradoxically, more avenues for influence may mean less control of the policy process in some instances. I return to this dilemma in Chapter Six.

In order to see the extent to which structural changes may have proceeded concomitantly with changes in audience and type, I constructed a set of categories that proved to be the least mechanical to employ, the most subject to dispute, but perhaps for those reasons, the most interesting as well. Documents were classified according to their structure of presentation. Those documents which manifested a discernible argument that moved logically from beginning to end *whether or not the argument convinced or was substantively sound* were coded "developed argument." Both Lincoln's laudatory first Inaugural Address and Buchanan's odious third State of the Union Address were so classified, for example. Documents that were structured by several arguments but not by an overall argument were classified "series of arguments." President Carter's "moral malaise" speech is of this character. While that speech announces an overall theme, it does not reveal an argument. On the other hand, unlike many of Carter's other speeches (and many recent presidential speeches generally), the "moral malaise" speech does not consist of a simple list of points strung together. "List of points" is the third classification. One clue to such a structure is paragraphing. Many speeches in the last two decades consist of single-sentence paragraphs, a structure that permits rearrangement almost at random without alteration of the "argument" of the speech. Single-sentence messages were coded "list of points." Finally, there are many speeches about which it is very hard to decide whether they represent a series of arguments *or* a list of points since they contain both structures. Speeches that were judged as less than 75 percent one category or the other were designated "mixed."

As indicated in Table 5.3, a greater percentage of nineteenth-century than twentieth-century messages are "developed" or "series" arguments. But also a greater percentage of nineteenth-century than twentieth-century messages are characterized as a list of points. Although statistically significant, these differences are slight. This distribution is misleading, however, because many nineteenth-century

TABLE 5.3 Structure of Communication in the Nineteenth
and Twentieth Centuries
(Percent and Number of Speeches Sampled)

Structure	Nineteenth Century		Twentieth Century	
	%	(N)	%	(N)
Developed argument	6	(20)	0	(0)
Series of arguments	19	(59)	11	(37)
List of points	61	(193)	55	(186)
Mixed (series and list)	15	(47)	34	(113)
Total	100	(319)	100	(336)

documents are one sentence "Special Messages" to Congress, letters reporting the transmittal of departmental reports. The reports
themselves are not included in the presidential papers (as they often
are in this century), perhaps due to a greater deference to Congress's
competing claim to authority over the bureaucracy at that time.

Table 5.4 gives a clearer picture of the structure of presidential
communications that actually sought to convey a message. All very
short documents (less than one-half page long) were deleted from the
samples of both centuries. Here the contrast is more striking than in
the larger sample. Seventy-five percent of nineteenth-century
speeches fall into the two "argument" categories, whereas ninety-
five percent of the twentieth-century speeches sampled have a "list"
or "mixed" character.

An examination of all inaugural and State of the Union addresses
(hereafter referred to as "Union Data") produces the same result. A
comparison of Table 5.5 with Table 5.3 shows a greater percentage
of the twentieth-century "Union Data" falling into the two argument
categories combined than do twentieth-century messages generally.
Yet the basic differences between the centuries persists. None of the
nineteenth-century messages in Table 5.5 were characterized as
"lists," versus 28 percent in the twentieth century.

TABLE 5.4 Structure of Communication in the Nineteenth
and Twentieth Centuries—Short Documents Deleted
(Percent and Number of Speeches Sampled)

	Nineteenth Century		Twentieth Century	
Structure	%	(N)	%	(N)
Developed argument	15	(12)	0	(0)
Series of arguments	60	(50)	5	(12)
List of points	7	(6)	50	(121)
Mixed (series and list)	18	(15)	45	(107)
Total	100	(83)	100	(240)

TABLE 5.5 Structure of Communication in
Inaugural Addresses and State of the Union Messages
(Percent and Number of Speeches Sampled)

	Nineteenth Century		Twentieth Century	
Structure	%	(N)	%	(N)
Developed argument	21	(30)	9	(10)
Series of arguments	74	(108)	18	(20)
List of points	0	(0)	28	(31)
Mixed (series and list)	6	(8)	45	(49)
Total	101	(146)	100	(110)

Finally, I examined one other indirect measure of the character of argument. I noted whether the documents contained any references to the Constitution (either the use of the word "Constitution" or reference to specific passages of the Constitution). I noted simply the presence or absence of mention, not number of mentions. It was thought that this classification might prove a rough measure of the presence or absence of constitutional argument. This rationale is not entirely satisfying, however, since the use of the word "Constitution" might occur without a constitutional argument, indeed might very well be a substitute for such an argument. With that caveat, note that only 4 percent of twentieth-century documents mention the Constitution, as against 11 percent in the earlier century. When very short documents are deleted from the sample, the figures are 5 percent for the twentieth century and 22 percent for the nineteenth. Looking at the "Union Data," 44 percent of the twentieth-century speeches mention the Constitution as against 87 percent of nineteenth-century messages.

While the differences between the centuries persist over each set of data, it is interesting to note, by comparing the random sample with the "Union Data," that developed argument, series of arguments, and mention of the Constitution are more likely to occur in current practice if the president is constrained by a traditional genre or form, such as the State of the Union Address. Thus, these twentieth-century speeches are a fitting metaphor for the larger political context in which presidents now find themselves, since they appear to be shaped by both doctrines, the old and the new.

The doctrinal prescriptions of each century and the estimates made of their persistence are simple. However, just as they rest upon theoretical complexity, as discussed earlier, they also point to complex political consequences that stem from and can be interpreted in light of the conjunction of these same systemic theories.

· 6 ·

LIMITS OF LEADERSHIP

Whatever doubts Americans may entertain about the wisdom of policies pursued by presidents, they no longer consider it inappropriate for presidents to attempt to move the public by programmatic speeches over the heads of Congress. The political successes of President Reagan, considered by many the nation's "great communicator," illustrate the contemporary legitimacy of Wilson's perspective. Judged by contemporary standards of leadership—Wilson's standards—Reagan's stewardship has been a model—that is, a "textbook" presidency. But how sound are the standards? What are the limits of the rhetorical presidency?

In actual textbooks on the modern presidency, instances of the successful use of popular appeals are highlighted, while instances of failure serve to further emphasize the qualities of character and skill that make the great leader and are apparently absent in the failed presidencies. Thus, Teddy Roosevelt's "swing" discussed in Chapter 4, Franklin Roosevelt's campaign to secure passage of the Social Security Act, and Eisenhower's television address in support of the Landrum-Griffin Act are all described, rightly, as models of popular leadership.[1] To be sure, these examples (and a very few others)

[1] See especially Elmer Cornwell, *Presidential Leadership of Public Opinion* (Bloomington: Indiana University Press, 1981), 24–26, 117–35.

were successes and are instructive as indications of conditions under which popular appeal was essential to the passage of proposed legislation.

Yet there is a danger in analyzing the failed presidential appeals solely in terms of these and like successes. By focusing upon the differences in presidential skill or character, for instance, one never examines the hypothesis that there are limits to popular leadership as an institutional practice or to the system's ability to function well under the auspices of a theory of popular leadership. There may be bounds to what even the most skillful presidents can accomplish under some circumstances—indeed, under "normal" circumstances.

The limits of the rhetorical presidency derive from features of our political system that are peculiarly American. As I suggested in Chapter 1, American political development may be usefully treated as a layered text. Basic structural features of the regime have not been substantially altered. Political reform has proceeded through reinterpretation of the Constitution rather than by replacement, or even significant amendment, of its structural principles. America has not faced the periodic revolutions that Jefferson prescribed nor recurrent changes of regime like those experienced in France. Wilson's reinterpretation of American politics altered elite and public understanding without changing the political logic that informed the original Constitution. Presidents inhabit an office structured by two systemic theories. Presidents are, as it were, caught between two layers of systemic thought, the product of a political hybrid.

The political tensions and contradictions induced by this hybrid are not the productive result of a deliberate act of political planning, like the tensions prescribed by the original theory of separation of powers, for example. Rather, they are the unintended byproducts of an incomplete reformation. The two theories of the constitution do not fit together to form a coherent whole. Instead, elements of the old and new ways frustrate or subvert each other.

Two case studies of presidential appeals over the heads of Congress illustrate the limits of the rhetorical presidency. Woodrow Wilson's campaign to found a League of Nations failed because he was compelled to speak in contradictory ways to different sorts of audiences—the Senate and the people at large—and his reponsibilities to speak to them were born of the political hybrid, the old and new ways. By refuting the common view that Wilson's failure was the result of a flawed personality, I can show how it rather reveals a limit of the system. "Credibility gaps," now common to presidential politics, might not be so much the defects of character as unintended consequences of the constitutional hybrid.

If elements of the old way frustrate the promise of the new in cases like Wilson's, Lyndon Johnson's War on Poverty campaign illustrates the power of the new way to subvert the old. Under some circumstances, the ability of the new way to aid a president in successfully getting what he wants may lead to long-term failure for the polity due to the breakdown of the deliberative process as a whole. The exclusion of Congress from its deliberative role may prevent consideration of the merits of policy. In cases like this one, the rhetorical presidency can be seen as subverter of the routines of governance rather than as a sign of a maturing democracy.

The Problem of Credibility: Woodrow Wilson and the League of Nations Campaign

At the end of the First World War and in the middle of his second term as president, Woodrow Wilson waged a vigorous losing battle to secure a peace treaty that had as its cornerstone a plan for a League of Nations. It is commonly thought among historians now that Wilson's own political activity contributed to (and perhaps was decisive in) preventing achievement of his highest political objectives. Wilson alienated the Senate by excluding it from the negotiating stage of the Treaty of Versailles, by refusing to compromise with Senate leaders who wished to amend the Treaty, and by rhetorically appealing "over the Senate's head" to the public at large. Moreover, Wilson's closest counselors and friends advised him to compromise with the

147

Senate because it was clear to them that Wilson's Senate support was far short of the two-thirds majority needed to ratify treaties. It was also clear to these advisers and other knowledgeable contemporaries that if Wilson would compromise on the wording of several provisions in the Treaty—which by Wilson's own account would not change the meaning of the Treaty, being only minor emendations—the Treaty would be ratified. Wilson refused to compromise. The Treaty was defeated.

With public sentiment behind the idea for a League of Nations, the Senate reconsidered the issue, reopening hearings and putting the matter to an unprecedented second vote. Again Wilson refused to compromise along the lines suggested by the senators, and the Treaty was defeated a second time. Historians and political analysts generally agree that Wilson's actions were the crucial causes of his own downfall—but for many years they have been perplexed about why Wilson acted as he did.

Any comprehensive explanation of the "why" of Wilson's behavior is bound to traverse several of the common sorts of explanation of strategic success or failure, problems of political or rhetorical skill, organization, or character. Since Wilson had proved extraordinarily successful at getting what he desired earlier in his presidency, scholars have not been content to rest their analyses of this final failure on lack of skill or ability alone. If Wilson had had such ability before the campaign, why did he lose it when it was most needed? Some of the best analyses of the episode have probed Wilson's character as the ultimate source of all of his difficulties. Examination of the most intelligent and influential example of these studies discloses difficulties characteristic of the personality approach.

The most thorough and erudite analysis of Wilson's personality was provided in 1956 by Alexander and Juliette George in *Woodrow Wilson and Colonel House*.[2] The Georges develop a subtle person-

---

[2] Alexander George and Juliette George, *Woodrow Wilson and Colonel House* (New York: Dover, 1964). See also Arthur S. Link, *Wilson the Diplomatist* (Baltimore: Johns Hopkins University Press, 1957), ch. 5.

ality theory to explain Wilson's political behavior, attempting to show how Wilson's thought, oratory, and actions were responses to deep psychic needs that were formed in his childhood. On first reading, the Georges' study appears to be a model of scholarly objectivity since they do not presuppose psychological explanations to be the only possible ones. Instead of beginning, as weaker analyses of political personality often do, with the assumption that personality is the key to explanation, they begin by attempting to see whether the political actor's own explanation of what he did is plausible. They attempt to think through Wilson's reasoning before rejecting it in favor of subrational or subconscious explanation. Moreover, they reinforce their own assessment of Wilson's activity with the common-sense reasoning of Wilson's contemporaries, most notably that of Colonel House.[3] Upon closer scrutiny, however, one discovers that the Georges fall short of the standards they set for themselves. The source of this difficulty, I shall argue, is their failure to illuminate the rhetorical features of Wilson's campaign, to distinguish the demands of rhetoric from the impulses of the psyche.

The crux of the argument from character is that Wilson's intransigent refusal to compromise with the Senate—that is, his refusal to attach reservations to the Treaty—was irrational and was the decisive cause of the defeat of the Treaty. Wilson's position was irrational because it is apparent to us now, and it was apparent to Wilson's contemporaries, that the suggested Senate reservations were so minor that they would not have altered the functioning of the League. Wilson himself conceded that the Senate reservations merely reiterated the plain meaning of the document. Moreover, while refusing to alter the document in any way, Wilson did agree to submit a set of "interpretations" virtually identical to the Senate "reservations," provided that these interpretations be in the form of a separate accompanying document—not part of the Treaty proper. As the Georges state the issue, "From start to finish, [Wilson] did not deviate one jot from his position. It was on this issue of the *form* of the reservations,

---

[3] See also Alexander George, "Assessing Presidential Character," *World Politics* 26 (January 1974): 10–30.

as well as the content of the final version of the reservation to Article X, that the whole Treaty foundered."[4]

Unless good reasons could be produced for insisting upon the form of the reservations, Wilson's intransigence must be considered irrational, and explained with the aid of psychological analysis. The sources of rhetoric that the Georges canvass are: the transcript of Wilson's famous meeting with the Senate Foreign Relations Committee, August 19, 1919; the texts of thirty-nine speeches Wilson delivered defending the Treaty, known as the "Western Tour" speeches; impromptu remarks quoted in contemporary press accounts; and the retrospective accounts of those close to Wilson (e.g., his wife).

From all of these sources, they unearth the following basic defense of the president's intransigence:

> Wilson based his refusal to have amendments or reservations embodied in the resolution of ratification on the grounds that such changes then would have to be approved by every nation—including Germany—which had signed the Treaty. Other nations, too, might follow our lead and start changing the Treaty. The floodgates would be thrown open, and the whole Treaty might have to be renegotiated. On the other hand, a separate statement of interpretations issued along with the resolution of ratification, the President held, would not require positive action on the part of the other signers of the contract.[5]

According to the Georges, this defense was irrational because it flew in the face of overwhelming contemporary evidence that the alleged difficulty was illusory or negligible. Senator Lodge and authorities in international law had argued that the Senate objections were in the form of reservations rather than amendments because only amendments required assent by the other signatories. Reservations would not have to be renegotiated because they could be accepted by silent acquiescence. They point out that these reservations would not have been considered obnoxious by our allies, because representatives of France and Great Britain indicated publicly that

[4] George and George, *Woodrow Wilson and Colonel House*, 284.
[5] Ibid.

they had no objections to the reservations, preferring a Treaty with reservations to no Treaty at all.[6] For these reasons, acceptance of Senate reservations would have had no appreciable effect upon the functioning of the League along the lines designed by Wilson. Why, then, did Wilson continue to insist that the Senate ratify the Treaty his way?

To answer that question, psychological theory is developed and extended. "Men require ways of expressing their aggressions and of protecting their self-esteem. Wilson's ways of doing both, unhappily, involved demanding his way to the letter and hurling himself against his opponents, no matter what the odds, no matter what the cost."[7] The details of the carefully developed theory need not concern us here. However, it is important to note the source and kind of evidence used to support the view that Wilson's problem with self-esteem prevented him from seeing his own enlightened interest. The Georges describe Wilson's Western Tour, in which he took his battle with the Senate directly to the people. In those speeches, Wilson not only repeated his argument to the Senate, he claimed that the Senate leadership was selfish, whereas he was principled; he claimed that he was convinced "that the overwhelming (majority of Senators) demand the treaty," that he was "certain of the outcome of the League fight," and that he was "simply an instrument of the people's will." Moreover, "the facts are marching and God is marching with them. You cannot resist them. You must either welcome them or subsequently, with humiliation, surrender to them. It is welcome or surrender. It is acceptance of great world conditions and great world duties or scuttle now and come back afterwards."

All of these statements, and statements like them, drawn from Wilson's public rhetoric, are taken at face value.[8] In other words, they argue that Wilson consciously believed all of these claims. Subconsciously, they argue, Wilson felt guilty about jeopardizing the Treaty, so he attempted to convince himself and the nation of his

[6] Ibid., 309.
[7] Ibid., 291.
[8] Ibid., especially 293–99.

moral superiority. Ironically, Wilson's technical arguments (e.g., those to the Senate Foreign Relations Committee) are treated as insincere, artfully contrived ''rationalizations,'' while his emotional appeals to the public are treated as consciously held beliefs, offered in sick, but nevertheless forthright, sincerity. An alternative view is that the technical arguments represent the core of Wilson's ''true beliefs'' and the emotional appeals are in many respects conscious exaggerations, designed to persuade and to make his prophecies self-fulfilling. In short, Wilson was trying to do the things that good rhetoricians are skilled at doing.

Let me now re-examine Wilson's position, drawing mainly on his presentation to the Senate Foreign Relations Committee, but also upon his public speeches. My object is not to demonstrate that Wilson was correct, but to indicate that his argument was weighty enough not to be regarded as irrational.

One must bear in mind that a politician may be motivated by selfishness, envy, greed, ambition, etc., and still be rational. Selfish men are often inhibited by the requirement that they create a reasonable defense of their position. As long as making a good argument is regarded as necessary, one's motive is irrelevant. It is only when selfishness (or whatever other motive) so dominates the mind that one does not care about the strength or merit of one's argument that one can be said to be irrational. The Georges adopt this criterion themselves, since they admit the possibility that Wilson's main opponent, Senator Lodge, was motivated by ambition and hatred of Wilson. What was most important, they note, was that Lodge was not blinded by his motives. They put the point in one instance as follows:

> It may be argued that Lodge's reservations were offensively worded. It may be argued that his motives in presenting them were questionable. But the reservations did not nullify the Treaty. They did not even seriously embarrass full participation of the United States in the League of Nations. In practice they would have been of little significance.[9]

[9] Ibid., 301. On the rational constraint of low motives, see *Federalist*, no. 1, p. 36.

On this view, Wilson was irrational because his motives obfuscated his political judgment. "His ambition, in other words, was compulsive. As a result, he found it difficult to pace his political demands prudently. . . . "[10]

Now consider Wilson's rhetoric to determine whether or not there is a plausible rational account of his position. Wilson met with Lodge's Foreign Relations Committee at the White House on August 19, 1919. We have a verbatim transcript of that meeting, and in it can be found the core of Wilson's defense.[11] Wilson began the meeting with a prepared statement that he said at the time was "entirely unreserved and plain-spoken." Not everything on Wilson's mind was spelled out, of course (nor on Lodge's either), but the impression one immediately gets from reading the record of this proceeding is that the arguments were remarkably candid and forthright. Moreover, very few of the rhetorical adornments that mark Wilson's public speeches can be found here.

After some introductory remarks thanking the committee for accepting his invitation to meet, the president began his plea with the thought that a speedy ratification of the Treaty was necessary. Due to postwar chaos, the United States economy was suffering, and there was growing unrest among some of the peoples of Europe who were uncertain as to their future. Nothing stood in the way of ratification except "certain doubts with regard to the meaning and implication of certain articles of the covenant of the League of Nations." Wilson reviewed the four major objections, or reservations, proffered by the Senate, indicating that each of these objections had been raised earlier by this same Senate committee at a meeting Wilson had had with them after completion of the first draft of the League Covenant. Wilson claimed to have carried those objections back to Paris and to have placed them before the Allies as suggested amendments to the Treaty. The Allies pointed out, and Wilson agreed with them, that

[10] Ibid., 320; see also George, "Assessing Presidential Character," 257.

[11] "Conference at the White House," April 19, 1919, reprinted as Appendix IV in Henry Cabot Lodge, *The Senate and the League of Nations* (New York: Charles Scribner's Sons, 1925), 297–379.

there was nothing in the Senate amendments that could not be deduced from the first draft of the Covenant itself. Nevertheless, Wilson insisted upon, and did get, the Senate amendments adopted.[12]

Wilson does not say here, but it is quite important, that he paid a great price for the Senate amendments.[13] He does point out to the Committee during the question period following his prepared remarks that the Allies accepted the Senate's interpretation, it being deducible from the Covenant itself, but they disagreed over the "wording" of the amendments. We know from records of the Treaty negotiations that Britain, France, Italy, and Japan all exacted concessions from Wilson—concessions that contradicted some of the principles of the League as well as some of Wilson's "Fourteen Points"—in exchange for their agreement to the Senate amendments. They might employ the same tactic again. For this reason and others, Wilson wished not to change any of the text of the Treaty. It is worth quoting his reasoning in full:

It has several times been suggested, in public debate and in private conference, that interpretations of the sense in which the United States accepts the engagements of the covenant should be embodied in the instrument of ratification. There can be no reasonable objection to such interpretations accompanying the act of ratification provided they do not form a part of the formal ratification itself. Most of the interpretations which have been suggested to me embody what seems to me the plain meaning of the instrument itself. But if such interpretations should constitute a part of the formal resolution of ratification, long delays would be the inevitable consequence, inasmuch as all the many governments concerned would have to accept, in effect, the language of the treaty before ratification would be complete. The assent of the German Assembly at Weimar would have to be obtained, among the rest, and I must frankly say that I could only with the greatest reluctance approach that assembly for permission to read the treaty as we understand it and as those who framed it quite certainly understood it. If the United States were to qualify the document in any way, moreover, I am confident from what I know of many conferences and de-

[12] Ibid., 297–302.

[13] George and George, *Woodrow Wilson and Colonel House*, 255 ff. Compare John Morton Blum, *Woodrow Wilson* (Boston: Little, Brown & Co., 1956), 175 ff.

bates which accompanied the formulation of the treaty that our example would immediately be followed in many quarters, in some instances with very serious reservations, and that the meaning and operative force of the treaty would presently be clouded from one end of its clauses to the other.[14]

In the discussion that ensued, Lodge suggested that reservations, unlike amendments, would not legally require explicit confirmations but could be confirmed by silent acquiescence. Wilson responded that there was some difference of opinion among authorities as to the legal issue whether or not explicit confirmation was required. That was not his point, but rather a political judgment that other nations would take advantage of the opportunity to offer their own reservations, which would "very much obscure our confident opinion as to how the Treaty was going to work."[15] Also, delay and uncertainty would result because given the criterion of silent acquiescence, we would not know whether all nations had agreed to the Treaty until their political activity in the League was sufficient to indicate that they did "agree" to the Treaty. (Perhaps affected by this reasoning, many Republican senators subsequently began to call for a requirement that the Treaty not go into effect until the reservations were *explicitly* confirmed by the other major signatories.)[16]

The president was not persuaded by the argument that the British and French had publicly announced their support of the reservations. Not only had many other nations *not* announced their support, but Wilson's experience from prior negotiation indicated to him that agreement to the "idea" was distinguished in the minds of Lloyd George and Georges Clemenceau from agreement to the "wording." As he put it, "I can testify that in our discussions in the commission on the League of Nations we did not discuss ideas half as much as we discussed phraseologies."[17]

Wilson's experience had taught him that general agreement on an

---

[14] "Conference," in Lodge, *Senate and League of Nations*, 302.

[15] Ibid., 311–13.

[16] George and George, *Woodrow Wilson and Colonel House*, 284.

[17] "Conference," in Lodge, *Senate and League of Nations*, 311.

interpretation of principle did not preclude haggling over specific formulations, and this had been used as a wedge to open the door for concessions from the United States. Wilson had at least a plausible argument when he contended that renegotiation would result if the Treaty were altered.

But the deepest argument was not the worry over renegotiation, or delay per se. It was rather a concern that equivocal support on the part of the United States would undermine the founding principles of the League. Repeatedly (in his remarks both to senators and to people at large), Wilson worried that the founding of the League proceed with an enthusiasm that did not call attention to "reservations." Known more as an idealist, few historians note that Wilson was preoccupied with the *problematic* character of the League of Nations. The League rested on nothing more than goodwill and the ability of each of its member nations to transcend national interest. "Unless you get the united, concerted purpose and power of the great governments of the world behind this settlement, it will fall down like a house of cards."[18] That power was military power only in the second instance; in the first instance it was the power of concerted opinion. And that opinion was not predicated on national interest, commonly understood, but rather on a concerted Kantian moral opinion that transcended national interest or utility.[19]

This lofty purpose was a fragile one. Wilson wished to avoid a situation in which the political practice of the United States contradicted the principles of the new League. For Wilson, the maxims that a nation should "be wise as serpents" and "guileless as doves" were incompatible, if one's nation was to be the prime mover in establishing a League of Nations.[20] His repeated exhortation that the League must either be accepted as is or be rejected can be seen as at least a

[18] Speech at Pueblo, Colorado, September 25, 1919, in Woodrow Wilson, *Public Papers of Woodrow Wilson*, ed. R. S. Baker and W. E. Dodd, 2 vols. (New York: Harper and Bros., 1927), 2:402.

[19] See, for example, "Conference," in Lodge, *Senate and League of Nations*, 307.

[20] Compare Kant, *Perpetual Peace*, ed. Lewis White Beck (New York: Bobbs Merrill, 1957), 35.

plausible argument when viewed against this background. United States hesitation would endanger the principled functioning of the League, since it would establish a founding precedent that each nation should interpret each responsibility as it saw fit. "We are not dealing with the kind of document which this is represented by some gentlemen to be; and inasmuch as we are dealing with a document simon-pure in respect of the very principles we have professed and lived up to, we have got to do one or other of two things—we have got to adopt it or reject it. There is no middle course. You cannot go in on a special privilege basis of your own. I take it that you are too proud to be exempted from responsibilities which the other members of the League will carry. We go in upon equal terms or we do not go in at all."[21] The contradiction between "special privilege" and the Kantian imperatives of the League is the meaning of Wilson's view that ratification with reservation was equivalent to "nullification."[22]

These reflections do not explore every feature of Wilson's argument, but they should provide sufficient explanation of the president's position on those issues deemed most problematic by the Georges. More importantly, they should be sufficient to establish a reasonable core to Wilson's behavior. This is not to establish that Wilson's position was better than his opposition's, merely that it was weighty enough to be considered rational.

But we are still left with the fact that Wilson failed to accomplish what he set out to do. If personality does not sufficiently account for his failure, what does? The hypothesis offered here is that the role of popular leader limited Wilson's political abilities and hindered his efforts. By focusing upon the role of popular leader I mean not to suggest that Wilson used popular rhetoric poorly, but that he used it well, and that the better he used it, the more difficult his political ef-

[21] Wilson, *Public Papers*, 2:402.

[22] The Georges may have missed this element of the argument by failing to take Wilson's moral claims seriously—those being Wilson's Kantian claims that a particular action is *right*, as distinct from prudential judgments regarding his or the nation's interests. Rather, the Georges put "right" in quotation marks, indicating its dubious status, and then proceed to treat the issue in their own terms. See, for example, *Woodrow Wilson and Colonel House*, 290, 319.

fort became. Wilson faced two rhetorical situations: (1) he needed to persuade senators to vote for the Treaty, and (2) he needed to persuade the citizenry to pressure senators to vote for the Treaty. The requisites of these two rhetorical situations contradicted each other; what was thought necessary to persuade senators would not work to persuade the people and vice versa.

We do not have reliable survey data regarding the state of public opinion towards the League or the Treaty. However, the political actors involved on both sides of the issue repeatedly claimed that public opinion was on "their side," suggesting that public opinion was in a state of uncertainty. There seems to have been a general disposition in favor of the idea of the League (it was endorsed in the campaign platforms of both major parties), but the public appeared to politicians to be uncertain whether they wanted *this* League as negotiated by Wilson. It also appears that the general disposition for some sort of League was not an issue of great intensity for most of the citizenry.[23] This is the kind of political climate that Wilson had long before argued most needs an orator-statesman. This kind of popular leader should be able to "interpret" the general disposition of the people, connect it to the practical proposal on the table, and intensify latent public support.[24]

But such a situation also makes leading senators formidable foes. Short of overwhelming public support for presidential policy, senators are, as constitutionally intended, insulated from the sort of pressure that the orator attempts to bring upon them. Wilson's peculiar difficulty was that he did not remake or refound the constitutional system, but instead reinterpreted it, engrafting a new role onto old institutions—institutions that had been fashioned on the basis of the old doctrine. Unless Wilson could gain the unequivocal support of the masses, his entreaties to them were likely to, and in fact did, alienate the Senate. Second, the sort of argument that was potentially

[23] Link, *Wilson the Diplomatist*, ch. 5.
[24] See especially Woodrow Wilson, *Leaders of Men*, ed. T. H. Vail (Princeton, N.J.: Princeton University Press, 1952).

the most persuasive to the people at large contradicted what senators had been told about the Treaty by Wilson.

The first problem, that of alienating the senators by turning the people against them, arose as Wilson strove to find the appeal to passion that would activate popular opinion, intensify it, bring it to expression. He could not leave his defense at a sober difference of opinion and expect the people to act. By the same token, Wilson was keenly sensitive to the need not to appear demogogic through unseemly name-calling or other tactics that might give his opposition an avenue to divert discussion away from the League and their inaction, to him and his character. Thus, Wilson carefully avoided singling out senators by name, except on one occasion toward the end of the tour, when he read from a speech by Lodge praising the idea of a League.[25] There Wilson tried to create a division as unobtrusively as is possible, while still being divisive. And at various other times he charged that those who disagreed with him must "not have read" the Treaty, must be "uninformed," or must have "personal motives," and must constitute a potentially "tyrannical minority."[26]

With respect to the charge of minority tyranny, Wilson often juxtaposed his remarks about the opposition to the Treaty with a discussion of the League's potential to thwart Bolshevism. On one occasion he explicitly disavowed that he was comparing his critics to Bolsheviks, but he did this in a way that reinforced the comparison. "Opposition is the specialty of those who are Bolshevistically inclined—and again, I assure you I am not comparing any of my respected colleagues to Bolshevists. I am merely pointing out that the Bolshevist lacks any spirit of constructiveness." Whether any of Wilson's immediate hearers were moved by the comparison is hard to discern, but senators certainly were. Toward the end of the tour, Wilson suggested another invidious comparison. Defeat of the League, he urged, would aid our enemy Germany. Thus those who urge defeat of the League, whether they intend to be or not, are allies

[25] Speech at San Diego, California, September 19, 1919, in Wilson, *Public Papers*, 2:283.

[26] Wilson, *Public Papers*, 2:199, 204, 210, 221, 264, 265.

of Germany. He noted the increase of pro-German propaganda in recent months.[27]

In addition to the problem of encouraging division, Wilson faced a credibility problem. The tone and direction of his remarks to the Senate differed from those to the people. To the Senate, as indicated above, Wilson's deepest argument was the thought that the League required an enthusiastic founding because it was inherently fragile, based only upon an as-yet-unformed international moral conscience. But to arouse the passionate support of the people, Wilson had to assure the public that an international moral conscience already existed, that one could safely deposit one's confidence in the League of Nations. Said Wilson:

[At Omaha, Nebraska:] Every great fighting nation in the world is on the list of those who are to constitute the League of Nations. I say every great nation, because America is going to be included among them, and the only choice, my fellow citizens, is whether we will go in now or come in later with Germany, whether we will go in as founders of this covenant of freedom or go in as those who are admitted after they have made a mistake and repented.[28]

[At Bismarck, North Dakota:] It seems very strange from day to day as I go about that I should be discussing the question of peace. It seems very strange that after six months of conference in Paris where the minds of more than twenty nations were brought together and where after the most profound consideration of every question and of every angle of every question concerned, an extraordinary agreement should have been reached—that while every other country concerned has stopped debating the peace, America is [still] debating it.[29]

[At Spokane, Washington:] Though the chance be poor is it not worth taking a chance? . . . As a matter of fact, I believe, after having sat in conference with men all over the world and found the attitude of their minds, the character of their purposes, that this [League] is a 99 percent insurance against war.[30]

[27] Ibid., 2:294, 117, 230, 10, 51.
[28] Ibid., 34.
[29] Ibid., 90.
[30] Ibid., 151.

It is more difficult to succeed with such rhetoric when popular leadership is legitimate than when it is not, for when it is legitimate it is generally thought (as Wilson had taught) that leaders can and ought to be candid and forthright in popular speech. It is thought that there is no difference between deliberative and popular oratory. On the other hand, when popular leadership is illegitimate, senators may more easily discount popular remarks as designed to move a crowd rather than to express official policy. Like the Georges, senators and other contemporaries of Wilson treated his popular rhetoric as a "true" position. From their vantage point, he had either lied to them, or his views were confused and contradictory.

The character of public opinion at the time, the rhetorical imperatives of different settings, and the special character of the proposed "Kantian" international organization made it perhaps impossible for Woodrow Wilson to speak his mind and found a League of Nations at the same time.

THE BREAKDOWN OF DELIBERATION: LYNDON JOHNSON'S WAR ON POVERTY

Lyndon Johnson's campaign for the Economic Opportunity Act of 1964 reversed the rhetorical practice of Woodrow Wilson's League fight. Instead of working out the merits of a technically complex program and then facing the difficult task of explaining it to the public in different, easily comprehended language, Johnson developed his popular rhetoric first. This popular rhetoric, well known as the "War on Poverty," contributed to the structuring of the legislation in the executive branch and served as a surrogate for deliberation at crucial junctures of the congressional process. The content of the poverty program was shaped, in large measure, by the "imperatives" or the "logic" of the War on Poverty rhetoric.

"War on Poverty" was a slogan devised by Kennedy staffers and used in the 1960 presidential campaign. There it did not elicit the supportive responses that were to come four years later when, in the

161

wake of Kennedy's assassination, Lyndon Johnson was able to turn the country's grief into a commitment to a moral crusade.[31]

The intellectual prehistory of the War on Poverty in the 1960–1963 period has been thoroughly explored by such scholars as James Sundquist, Sar Levitan, and Daniel Moynihan.[32] While this prehistory of theories and strategies to ameliorate the poverty problem did create a disposition among some White House staffers to address the issue, its major influence occurred after passage of the legislation, as poverty workers sought to make sense of their mission. For the present purpose of examining the development and enaction of the legislation, it is important to note that while some private groups had begun to implement new theories of social reform, and while some Ford Foundation-sponsored groups "ultimately provided an arsenal of weapons for the war on poverty . . . it is fair to say that the arsenal was not really discovered until *after* the decision to declare war was made."[33]

Kennedy's Council of Economic Advisors had created a study group on poverty, but Kennedy did not encourage the development of draft legislation until about a month before he died. And it was not until November 19 that Kennedy gave Walter Heller, Chairman of the CEA, "a flat 'yes' " to develop a package of anti-poverty measures for the 1964 legislative program. Heller had canvassed the government for specific proposals "to prevent entry into poverty, to promote exits from poverty, and to alleviate the difficulties of persons who cannot escape from poverty." He received fifty-eight proposals

[31] John Bibby and Roger Davidson, *On Capitol Hill* (New York: Holt, Rinehart and Winston, 1967), 224. For a particularly insightful legislative history, see Richard Blumenthal, "The Bureaucracy: Anti-Poverty in the Community Action Program," in *American Political Institutions and Public Policy* ed. Allan P. Sindler (Boston: Little, Brown & Co., 1969), 128–79.

[32] James L. Sundquist, *Politics and Policy* (Washington, D.C.: The Brookings Institution, 1968), 111–34; Sar A. Levitan, *The Great Society's Poor Law* (Baltimore: Johns Hopkins University Press, 1969), 3–18; Daniel Patrick Moynihan, *Maximum Feasible Misunderstanding* (New York: Free Press, 1970).

[33] Sundquist, *Politics and Policy*, 135. Most of the scholars examining the War on Poverty continue to employ the war metaphor in their analyses!

and was in the midst of reviewing them when "word of the assassination came from Dallas." Two days later Heller reported on the incipient project to Lyndon Johnson, who is reported to have said, "That's my kind of program . . . move full speed ahead."[34]

At this point, the need for a rhetorical campaign supplanted the technical legislative work of the staff of the CEA as the conceptual focus of the project. Distilling thirty-five proposals out of the fifty-eight suggestions, Bureau of the Budget staff " 'floundered,' as one participant put it, in search of a theme and a *rationale* that would distinguish the new legislation, as dramatically as possible, from all that had gone before—the Area Redevelopment Act, MDTA, Appalachia, the Public Welfare Amendments of 1962, the youth employment program, the pending proposal for [a domestic peace corps] and all the rest."[35] The solution found was two-fold: the idea of community action was abstracted from work by the President's Committee on Juvenile Delinquency and Youth Crime. The basic idea was to disperse federal funds to local community "development corporations," who would "plan the programs, expend the funds, and provide the coordinating mechanism." This solution provided a visible new entity to focus attention on the problem of poverty while postponing serious discussion of how the money was to be spent.[36]

The second way in which the poverty program was to be distinguished from previous programs was its package—a massive rhetorical campaign designed to "emphasize a sense of urgency about starting a war on poverty."[37] The key element was that the impoverished would be singled out for attention, rather than being one group among several to directly benefit from a program. A billion dollars was included in the budget, with half designated for programs to be determined by community action groups and the rest for other appropriations to be administered by those same groups. More im-

[34] Ibid., 137; see also Lyndon Johnson, *The Vantage Point* (New York: Holt, Rinehart and Winston, 1971), 71.

[35] Sundquist, *Politics and Policy*, 137.

[36] Levitan, *Great Society*, 18.

[37] Ibid.

portantly, Johnson made the program the most visible theme of his first State of the Union message.

> This administration today, here and now, declares unconditional war on poverty in America. I urge this Congress and all Americans to join with me in that effort. . . .
>
> It will not be a short or easy struggle, no single weapon or strategy will suffice, but we shall not rest until the war is won. . . .
>
> Poverty is a national problem, requiring improved national organization and support. But this attack, to be effective, must also be organized at the State and local level and be supported by State and local efforts. . . .
>
> Our aim is not only to relieve the symptoms of poverty, but to cure it, and above all prevent it. . . .[38]

Although only the vague decision regarding the community action structure had been made, in his speech Johnson listed eleven possible programs, such as the Domestic Peace Corps, a broader food stamp program, altered minimum-wage laws, and the building of more libraries, hospitals and nursing homes. At least half of these proposed efforts did not find their way directly into the War on Poverty package. The important theme of the message was not the programs themselves (none of which were defended there) but the simple declaration of war. The metaphor of war not only structured or provided the form for that section of the speech, it constituted its meaning as well. For example, Johnson stated, "Our chief weapons in a more pinpointed attack will be better schools and better health, and better training and better job opportunities to help more Americans. . . ." There is nothing new or unusual about the desire for "better health"—all presidents and all Americans are "for" those things; what would be new was that the specific programs funded to achieve these objectives (many of which were then pending as individual initiatives before Congress) would now be part of a *war*.

In place of an argument indicating why poverty should be consid-

---

[38] Lyndon Johnson, "Annual Message to Congress on the State of the Union," January 8, 1964, in Lyndon B. Johnson, *Public Papers of the President of the United States 1963–64*, 2 vols. (Washington, D.C.: U.S. Government Printing Office, 1965), 1:112.

ered a national problem, why it required a coordinated program, why present efforts were insufficient or ill-conceived, and why the kinds of legislation suggested by the president fit together as a single program—instead of this, the president offered a metaphor, whose premise provided the answers. If we were at *war* with poverty, such an effort would require a national mobilization, coordination, extensive executive discretion, and the potential involvement of virtually any social program as vital to the war effort. Wars require these things. Under the Constitution, only Congress can "declare" an actual war, presumably after its need has been deliberated upon and publicly established. The president declared the War on Poverty, and as we shall see, the executive branch and Congress then proceeded as if the need and its rationale had been established.

Before Congress could act and the people enlist, the president had to draft the legislation. For a month and a half after the State of the Union message, the Budget Bureau, CEA, and White House staffs attempted to fashion a program of community action; but they faced the problem that, though there was private program experience with the strategy through several community action programs in Manhattan, New Haven, and elsewhere, the idea had only been seized upon by the president's men in late December under the pressure of a deadline for an "idea" for the State of the Union message. *"They did not know and had no time to find out exactly how community action was in fact working."*[39] Disputes then developed over whether to emphasize working through existing local agencies or creating new ones, whether to emphasize planning or programs, and whether to emphasize programs directed at youth, health, and education or programs directed to problems of "structural unemployment."[40]

Partly to provide a fresh opinion, partly to give a potential director of the program the opportunity to fashion it, partly to further capitalize upon the public attention given the emerging program, Johnson appointed Sargent Shriver as his assistant in charge of poverty programs and gave him the specific responsibility to draft the legisla-

[39] Sundquist, *Politics and Policy*, 140.
[40] Ibid., 142.

165

tion.[41] Once appointed, Shriver canvassed the executive departments again and contacted hundreds of community leaders for their suggestions (on stationery that was emblazoned "Task Force on the War on Poverty"). Many of the community leaders were contacted less for their ideas (for time did not permit reflection upon them) than for their support of the "war."

Shriver put together an extensive six-title legislative package in *six weeks*. Again, the primary conceptual constraints were not those of competing theories of social reform (although inevitably every program reflected such theories), nor was Shriver burdened by the need to resolve tensions between competing theories of executive organization (although such disputes arose). Rather, the primary problem was to fashion a program that fit Johnson's rhetoric while it adhered to his budget ceiling. Given the budget ceiling, one program, the community action idea, could not show enough significant "victories" to constitute a nation seriously at war, but it was thought that an effort with five or six visible programs might indeed appear to be a warlike effort.[42] Moreover, even if a community action program could be funded well, even massively, Johnson had pledged to coordinate all sorts of projects and actually named several in his message. As James Sundquist has stated, "The President and the Press had by this time built up expectations so vast that a one-idea, one-title bill [devoted to community action] would be a serious letdown. The very idea of a massive coordinated attack on poverty suggested mobilizing under that banner all or as many as possible of the weapons that would be used."[43]

The six-week effort produced a greatly expanded bill. The one-title bill now had six, and the Community Action Program was joined by some half dozen other major projects, some of which had been rejected previously by Congress, and others of which were under

[41] Bibby and Davidson, *On Capitol Hill*, 231.

[42] Sundquist, *Politics and Policy*, 141.

[43] Sundquist, *Politics and Policy*, 142; see Moynihan, *Maximum Feasible Misunderstanding*, and J. David Greenstone and Paul Peterson, *Race and Authority in Urban Politics* (New York: Russell Sage, 1976).

consideration as separate bills pending before the Congress. Among the added programs were: a "Job Corps" to provide training and remedial education to the unskilled urban poor; a Neighborhood Youth Corps; a college work-study program; and Adult Basic Education Program; a rural loan program; a small business loan program; and a "Domestic Peace Corps," which came to be known as VISTA.

The projects and priorities of the Community Action Program were left undefined, and the director of the proposed coordinating agency—the Office of Economic Opportunity—was given discretion to determine which proposals "give promise of progress toward the elimination of poverty through developing employment opportunities, improving human performance, motivation, and productivity, and bettering the conditions under which people live, learn and work." This title also stipulated that the program be administered "with the maximum feasible participation of residents of the areas." This condition became the subject of tremendous political controversy when the legislation was implemented, and of scholarly controversy after that.[44] The meaning of the phrase was not discussed either by Shriver's people or by congressmen during the "deliberation" on the program. Yet again, it must be noted that the phrase is not as controversial if, like the rest of the bill, it is understood in terms of the rhetorical campaign rather than in terms of the merits of the program. Johnson had called for assistance from all the citizenry in the war effort; wars require "maximum feasible participation."

The bill was accompanied by the President's Special Message to the Congress Proposing a Nationwide War on the Sources of Poverty.[45] As is customary, the message was a written one and was formally addressed "to the Congress of the United States," not to the people at large. Yet the message was written as if it were a popular speech, designed to arouse a general disposition of support (like the State of the Union Message) rather than provide a careful defense of the proposals suggested. It could not draw upon a reasoned defense

[44] See Greenstone and Peterson, *Race and Authority*, and Moynihan, *Maximum Feasible Misunderstanding*.
[45] Johnson, *Public Papers, 1964–65*, 1:375–80.

for the proposals because as of then (March 16, 1964) there was no clear rationale developed in the executive branch apart from the president's previous rhetoric.

Johnson's message to Congress was written in a style and format that had been developed by speechwriters for popular addresses. That style, adopted by all presidents since Johnson, emphasizes short paragraphs (many a single sentence) to provide easy excerpts for the evening news, which itself is organized around thirty-second or one-minute segments.[46] The structure makes it more likely that the news will report a catchy phrase. Many of these speeches could be rearranged randomly by paragraph without much distortion of their meaning; they are generally not developed arguments.

Rather than provide a reasoned defense of the policies proffered, Johnson's message appears to have had two objectives: to further inspire the populace, and to announce the components of the legislative package in prose more acceptable than the legal form of the bill itself—in other words, to restate the bill. With respect to the first objective consider the following section of the message:

> The path forward has not been an easy one,
> But we have never lost sight of our goal: an America in which every citizen shares all the opportunities of his society, in which every man has a chance to advance his welfare to the limit of his capacities.
> We have come a long way toward this goal.
> We still have a long way to go.
> The distance that remains is the measure of the great unfinished work of our society.
> To finish that work I have called for a national war on poverty. Our objective: total victory.[47]

The message is written as if Johnson was appearing before a teleprompter, but again this was a written message to Congress. After stating the six basic titles of the bill, and indicating his intention to appoint Sargent Shriver as director of the proposed Office of Eco-

---

[46] Reagan is a partial exception. Many of his speeches do not manifest this form, although some do. See the discussion of Reagan in Chapter 7 below.

[47] Johnson, *Public Papers, 1964–65*, 1:375–80.

nomic Opportunity ("my personal Chief of Staff for the War against poverty"), Johnson asks for "immediate action on all these programs," and concludes with a thousand word development of the war metaphor.

> What you are being asked to consider is not a simple or an easy program. But poverty is not a simple or easy enemy.
>
> It cannot be driven from the land by a single attack on a single front. Were this so we would have conquered poverty long ago.
>
> Nor can it be conquered by government alone. . . .
>
> . . . [This program] will also give us a chance to test our weapons, to try our energy and ideas and imagination for the many battles yet to come. As conditions change and as our experience illuminates our difficulties, we will be prepared to modify our strategy. . . .
>
> On similar occasions in the past we have been called upon to wage war against foreign enemies which threatened our freedom. Today we are asked to declare war on a domestic enemy which threatens the strength of our nation and the welfare of the nation.[48]

With this message, Johnson launched a sophisticated publicity campaign that included personal visits to poverty-stricken regions by the Johnson family and appeals to political, social, and economic organizations to assist in spreading the message. "Help was asked of everyone from the Daughters of the American Revolution to the Socialist Party. The United Auto Workers called for a 'Citizens' Drive on Poverty'; the Urban League announced its own 'war on poverty.'. . ."[49]

The public pressure was matched with shrewd parliamentary judgment in presenting the bill to Congress. Johnson's bill was of the "omnibus" variety, containing programs that individually had been the proper province of four or five committees of each house. Johnson arranged for the House and Senate Labor Committees to each create new ad hoc subcommittees for the poverty program. House Labor Committee chairman Adam Clayton Powell chaired his own subcommittee, which he named the "Subcommittee on the War on

[48] Ibid.

[49] Elinor Graham, "Poverty and the Legislative Process," in *Poverty as a Public Issue*, ed. Ben B. Seligman (New York: Free Press, 1965).

Poverty Program,'' thereby inscribing an acceptance of the rhetorical premise of the legislation in the formal purpose of the committee.

The committee began hearings the day after the Special Message, with virtually no staff preparation. Those hearings (which were the main focus of the activity of both houses) lasted about a month, with fifty-six witnesses questioned favoring the bill, four of no opinion, and nine against. ''The hearings were designed to advertise broad support for the poverty bill.''[50] Shriver testified and was followed by seven cabinet secretaries, including the secretary of defense, called ostensibly because proposed Job Corps centers would be housed in surplus military facilities. Throughout these hearings and the very brief Senate hearings that followed (five witnesses, four ''for'' and one ''against''), the questions dealt with material tangential to the basic merits of the program. ''At no point did the Republicans attack the bill head on.''[51] Efforts were made by Republicans to woo Southern Democrats away from supporting the bill by suggesting that the program would bypass governors, and race prejudice was appealed to by suggesting that the Job Corps centers would have to be integrated. But when fundamental questions regarding the rationale of the poverty program were raised, witnesses provided (and got away with only providing) answers deduced from the war metaphor rather than an articulation of the merits of particular proposals. For example, Congressman Frelinghuysen, the senior Republican member from New Jersey, questioned Secretary Celebreze of HEW:

[Frelinghuysen:] What is the difference in emphasis between what your Department is responsible for [now] and what the new agency is responsible for? To my mind, this new agency [OEO] is another authority superimposed above the authority of your department with respect to [your Department's] responsibilities.

[Celebreze:] First let me say that in working up the program there was close coordination between my Department and Sargent Shriver. As a matter of fact, part of my staff was in constant communication with him. . . . Most of our programs, eventually may affect the economic status of many individuals. But these programs, as they now exist, are

[50] Bibby and Davidson, *On Capitol Hill*, 238.
[51] Sundquist, *Politics and Policy*, 145.

aimed at one specific project. They have their limitations. If we are sincere, if our attitude is that we must have a war on poverty, and that is the name used, the war on poverty, then it becomes evident that if we are going to make a concerted attack on all the many elements that go into the poverty program. . . . There ought to be unification under one head if we wanted to have a war on poverty.

If you are going to declare war, you have to have one general of the Army, you cannot have six generals.[52]

Much of the "deliberation" over the bill was of this character: OEO would be given authority to coordinate, because wars require central coordination, close to the president; Shriver would be given discretion to develop criteria for acceptance of community action programs because war requires discretion and flexibility to change strategies; rural farm loan programs and urban Head Start centers would be coordinated by the same chief of staff because the enemy is lurking everywhere and wears different guises. Frelinghuysen was one of a very few congressmen to note and complain of the dominance of the metaphor, but his complaints found no sympathetic hearers, so he too began to reason in terms of the war metaphor. As one Republican lamented during the floor debate, " 'War on Poverty' is a terrific slogan, particularly in an election year. It puts doubters under the suspicion of being in favor of poverty."[53] Moreover, it puts doubters under the suspicion of being unpatriotic, immoral, or both. Faced with this rhetorical problem, some Republicans mounted a rhetorical counteroffensive that further detracted from consideration of the program's merits. If Johnson's program could not be attacked because of its moral and patriotic premises, perhaps Johnson himself could be depicted as hypocritical or immoral in light of his own rhetoric.

Two Republican Congressmen . . . made a well publicized flying tour of Mrs. Lyndon Johnson's Alabama farm—which they described as a "pocket of poverty." They returned to display photographs of the six Negro sharecroppers and tenants living on the Johnson land, and to say

[52] Hearings, Subcommittee on War on Poverty, 88th Cong., 2nd Sess., Pt. I, pp. 138–39; see also p. 190.
[53] Representative Charles B. Hoovar of Iowa, *Congressional Record*, vol. 110 (August 6, 1964), p. 18315, quoted in Sundquist, *Politics and Policy*, 145.

that, "We saw people living in deplorable poverty, with little evidence of concern by their millionaire landlords."[54]

White House statements rebutted the charge, preventing it from capturing too much attention. While the White House could and did attempt to show that Johnson had been inaccurately characterized, they could not claim the tactic to be improper given the rhetorical war they had begun.

By late summer the bill had passed both Houses of Congress and was signed by the president with only a handful of insignificant amendments added by Congress. The victory was larger than expected in the House (226 to 185) and was as large as expected in the Senate (61 to 34). It was the first of the Great Society programs, and the political "clout" revealed by Lyndon Johnson helped pave the way for more domestic legislation. James Sundquist has written, "Whatever history may judge to have been its legislative merits, the political merits of the war on poverty in 1964 cannot be denied."[55] That is true only if one sees no important connection between the form political tactics take and the quality of the legislation that results. The same popular rhetoric that provided clout for victory substituted passionate appeal and argument by metaphor for deliberation. Johnson's tactic not only produced a hastily packaged program, his clear victory ensured that he and not Congress would be blamed if the program failed. And fail it did. As David Zarefsky shows in his perceptive study of the implementation of the Act, ". . . The very choices of symbolism and argument which had aided the adoption of the program were instrumental in undermining its implementation and in weakening public support for its basic philosophy."[56]

[54] Bibby and Davidson, *On Capitol Hill*, 242. A poor tenant of Mrs. Johnson's showed loyalty to his landlord by refusing an offer by these Congressmen to personally pay to fix his roof. *The New York Times*, May 29, 1964, p. 9.

[55] Sundquist, *Politics and Policy*, p. 145.

[56] David Zarefsky, *President Johnson's War on Poverty* (University: University of Alabama Press, 1986), xii.

· 7 ·

DILEMMAS OF GOVERNANCE

Most scholars of the presidency have adopted implicit or explicit criteria of change in American politics. Distinguishing between development and metamorphoses, students of the presidency have nearly all regarded the rhetorical presidency as a logical and benign growth of the institution rather than a fundamental transformation of it. That basic postulate is wrong. The rhetorical presidency signals and constitutes a fundamental transformation of American politics that began at the outset of the twentieth century.

However, while the historical and statistical materials presented here indicate that the Wilsonian doctrine is ascendant, those materials also reveal the persistence of founding principles. Those founding principles still lie behind the constitutional structures that shape our highest office. In many ways, presidents still act just as presidents always have—as constitutional officers, not popular leaders. Or, if they do not so act, they must confront other political actors who do. The modern presidency is thus a hybrid. While structural features of the institution continue to embody founding doctrine, and while emergency or crisis appeals to public opinion in the manner of Theodore Roosevelt can be justified as consistent with the founding perspective, the Wilsonian view has replaced the founders' as the basic underpinning of presidential self-understanding and public legitimacy. For these reasons the idea that the rhetorical presidency represents a transformation of American politics stands somewhere in the middle of a spectrum that extends from ''change'' (as logical growth or development) on one side to ''revolution'' (as refounding or total restructuring) on the other.

Many of the dilemmas and frustrations of the modern presidency may be traced to the president's ambivalent constitutional station, a vantage place composed of conflicting elements. In this final chapter I present a series of reflections upon the meaning and significance of the transformation of American politics wrought by the rhetorical presidency. After discussing the character of the basic dilemmas revealed by the president's peculiar station today, I indicate briefly how the development of parties and campaigns, the mass media, and the speechwriting apparatus in the White House reflects and reinforces the basic governmental dilemmas. I discuss President Reagan's leadership as exemplary of the rhetorical presidency and show how his campaigns for tax reform, budget cuts, and the strategic defense initiative recapitulate the dilemmas earlier illustrated by the leadership of Teddy Roosevelt, Woodrow Wilson, and Lyndon Johnson. I conclude by indicating why rhetorical leadership poses difficulties for modern constitutional rule.

CRISIS POLITICS AND NORMAL POLITICS

Placed in an ambivalent office, the product of two theories of the constitutional order, contemporary presidents inevitably find that rhetorical strategies do not always work as expected, nor are they cost-free as the conventional wisdom implies. Presidents may be thwarted by other political actors, as was President Wilson in his League of Nations campaign, or by conflicting demands of the presidency itself born of the institution's hybrid character. President Carter, for example, opened himself to charges of hypocrisy and consequent public disenchantment three months after the ''moral ma-

174

laise'' address in which he eschewed the constitutional role of ''head of government'' in favor of the Wilsonian ''leader of the people.'' Faced with the Iranian hostage crisis, the president retreated into the White House out of public view in order to act ''presidential,'' which is to say more as head of government than as leader of the people. From the point of view of presidents or presidential strategists, the rhetorical presidency is more dilemma-ridden than is usually acknowledged.[1]

Dilemmas inherent in the rhetorical presidency are also apparent when one adopts a larger, more systemic perspective, that of institutional theorist rather than of presidential strategist. From this perspective it must be acknowledged that the presidency is more energetic than it was in the nineteenth century, that it is more capable of leading comprehensive social change, and that it has maintained a public legitimacy that it might not have maintained if other features of the system had become more democratic and it had not.

Woodrow Wilson's critique of the original Constitution contains a number of insights that cannot be dismissed. The pursuit of ''extensive and arduous'' enterprises that the founders noted as a great benefit to derive from a unitary, energetic, executive may not have been possible for some projects in the twentieth century without popular leadership. The rhetorical presidency appears to be a reasonable extension of executive power to the extent that it is necessary to effect such constitutionally legitimate enterprises as the New Deal.[2] Energy, the possibility of social change, and democratic legitimacy were insufficiently fulfilled promises of the original Constitution.

Synoptic change, as distinct from incremental policy, seems to re-

[1] *Washington Post*, July 14, 15, 16, 1979, p. 1. Compare Samuel Kernell, *Going Public: New Strategies of Presidential Leadership* (Washington, D.C.: CQ Press, 1986), 227: ''As one looks to the future, the prospect for the continued use of going public as presidential strategy looks bright.''

[2] Cf. Theodore Lowi, *The Personal President* (Ithaca, N.Y.: Cornell University Press, 1985). Lowi's important study of plebiscitary presidential leadership, being almost unequivocal in its criticism, requires, and contains, an argument that the New Deal was unconstitutional.

quire an executive energized by a direct relation to the people.[3] To see that this is so, consider an intelligent next step to an argument that asserts that the rhetorical presidency is unequivocally bad, and entirely inconsistent with the promise of the original Constitution. To attempt a return to the better "old way" would be a reasonable next step for one who did not see plebiscitary leadership as a dilemma. How would one return to an earlier polity, and who would bring us there? Wouldn't we need to be led by one regarded as the legitimate spokesman for the nation as a whole—that is, by a president appealing to us directly? This is a hypothetical version of the true story presented in Chapter 4, where I described Theodore Roosevelt's attempt to restore founding principles through popular leadership. Refounding or restorative leadership, even in the service of the "old way," seems to require practices proscribed in the nineteenth century.

Yet these systemic benefits have brought with them systemic costs, among them an increasing lack of "fit" between institution and occupant, a greater mutability of policy, an erosion of the processes of deliberation, and a decay of political discourse. The historical materials presented earlier illustrate these observations.

The general problem of "fit" between institution and occupant is not new, but its character has changed. Within the practices shaped by the founders' doctrine, such a problem was more likely to arise in times of crisis, where exceptional leadership could not be ensured and, if fortuitously found, would need to transcend the normal institutional arrangements. The founders' office was structured for "normal"—that is, undistinguished—men. The institutional arrangements supplied "the defects of better motives." The premise of the structure was that "enlightened statesman would not always be at the helm."[4] Thus, qualities dependent upon individual talent, like eloquence, found little doctrinal support, while those that could be made

---

[3] For a good discussion of the merits of synoptic versus incremental policymaking, see Jennifer Hochschild, *The New American Dilemma* (New Haven, Conn.: Yale University Press, 1985).

[4] *Federalist*, no. 10, p. 80.

general or common, like "constitutional authority," were given prominence. This point was well understood by James Bryce, the British political scientist who made a Tocqueville-like tour of the United States in the 1880s. In an essay entitled "Why Great Men Are Not Chosen Presidents," he stated:

> Eloquence, whose value is apt to be overrated in all free countries, imagination, profundity of thought or extent of knowledge, are all in so far a gain to a President that they make him a bigger man, and help him to gain a greater influence over the nation, an influence which, if he be a true patriot he may use for its good. But they are not necessary for the due discharge in ordinary times of the duties of his post. A man may lack them and yet make an excellent President.[5]

Under the auspices of the Wilsonian doctrine, all presidents labor under the expectation of great oratory. Since there is no reason to expect that more politicians are capable of great oratory now than in the century of Clay, Webster, and Randolph, it is increasingly the case that presidential abilities and institutional requirements diverge. Moreover, since the office still requires occupants who possess the traditional political skills, the likelihood of securing men or women with all requisite talents is still less. Because the requirements of the station were fewer, the founders could claim a "moral certainty that the office of President will seldom fall to the lot of any man who is not in an eminent degree endowed with the requisite qualifications."[6] If that were ever true, it is less so now.

With respect to the second issue, both the founders and Wilson saw that mutability of law or policy might lead to decreased respect for law in general. While the founders expressed a greater reluctance toward change of any sort and particularly toward constitutional change than did Wilson, the twentieth-century doctrine is not hospitable to all kinds of change. Wilson's doctrine rests upon a view of "progressive" change, or change that follows a pattern presaged in

---

[5] James Bryce, *The American Commonwealth* (1885, reprint edition, New York: G. P. Putnam's Sons, 1959), 27–34. See also Nelson Polsby, "Against Presidential Greatness," *Commentary* (January 1977).

[6] *Federalist*, no. 69, p. 414.

prior developments. For Wilson, mutability would be a serious problem if the changes in law frustrated or retarded the movement of history.

The rhetorical presidency makes change, in its widest sense, more possible. Because complex arrangements of policies are packaged and defended as wholes (e.g., the New Freedom, New Deal, Great Society, New Federalism, War on Poverty, etc.), they are more likely to be rejected as wholes. Reagan's substantial ''supply side'' successes, for example, represent a repudiation of nearly all the Great Society programs enacted just fifteen years ago. If in the near future some visible portion of the Reagan ''package'' should fail, it is more likely that his entire constellation of policies will be reversed than would have been the case if, as in the nineteenth century, policy merits had a greater role than policy slogan in structuring debate and decision. An important point here is not only that disrespect for law will ensue, but also that valuable policies will continually be discarded along with those obviously flawed.

As the War on Poverty illustrates, the more the rhetorical presidency succeeds as a strategy in the short term, the more likely it is that deliberative processes will be eroded. Today the pace of policy development follows less the rhythms of Congress and more the dynamics of public opinion. The consequence of this development is not only that Congress will often be left out of the deliberative stages of policy formation and that rhetorical imperatives will play a large role, but also that Congress will be forced to respond in kind. Television and radio networks now regularly provide for congressional response—actually, opposition party response—to presidential speeches, including the State of the Union Address. Crafted as popular appeals before receipt of the president's messages, these congressional speeches are beamed to the people over the head of the president. With television now introduced into the Senate and House, we face the very real prospect of our two political branches talking past each other to a vast amorphous constituency.

This surfeit of speech by politicians constitutes a decay of political discourse. It replaces discussion structured by the contestability of opinion inherent to issues with a competition to please or manipulate the public.[7] As the Johnson case illustrates, the rhetorical presidency enhances the tendency to define issues in terms of the needs of persuasion rather than to develop a discourse suitable for the illumination and exploration of real issues—that is, problems that do not depend upon the certification of a public opinion poll to be recognized as needful of examination. It is increasingly the case that presidential speeches themselves have become the issues and events of modern politics rather than the medium through which issues and events are discussed and assessed. Subsequent speeches by presidents and other politicians often continue to elaborate the fictive world created in the initial address, making that world, unfortunately, a constitutive feature of "real" national politics.[8]

When speech is designed to appeal to public opinion, especially in oral, visible performance, the effect upon political discourse is more troublesome than a transient arousal of passion in the demos. More significantly, the terms of discourse that structure subsequent "sober" discussion of policy are altered, reshaping the political world in which that policy and future policy is understood and implemented. By changing the meaning of policy, rhetoric alters policy itself and the meaning of politics in the future.

A number of historians have traced many of the excesses of Cold War anti-communism to a single presidential appeal, the Truman Doctrine speech. While the evidence is not conclusive, it is not sufficient to reject their arguments, as Samuel Kernell has done, simply because public opinion polls do not display a marked change in anticommunist sentiments immediately following the speech.[9] Instead,

---

[7] Benjamin Ginsberg, *The Captive Public* (New York: Basic Books, 1986). Cf. Benjamin I. Page and Robert Y. Shapiro, "Presidents as Opinion Leaders: Some New Evidence," *Policy Studies Journal* 12 (June 1984): 647–62, and idem, "Effects of Public Opinion on Policy," *American Political Science Review* 77 (March 1983): 175–90.

[8] To be sure, nineteenth-century rhetoric contained fictive aspects, and contemporary rhetoric requires some connection to a world outside of itself. I mean to emphasize what *The Federalist* calls "the aptitude and tendency" of constitutional arrangements. *Federalist*, no. 69, p. 414.

[9] Walter LaFeber, *America, Russia, and the Cold War, 1945–1971*, 2nd ed. (New York: John Wiley, 1972); Charles Bohlen, *The Transformation of American Foreign Policy* (New York: Norton, 1969); Joyce Kolko and Gabriel Kolko, *The Limits of*

one needs to explore the extent to which the terms of the speech shaped subsequent elite debate, journalistic coverage, and congressional deliberation. (One must be attentive to the *way* policy is discussed, not just to the aggregate ''preferences'' expressed or ''stands'' taken.) Each of these arenas is, of course, overdetermined, but the War on Poverty case illustrates the power of the rhetorical presidency to alter the terms of political discourse.[10]

The steep decline in constitutional speech noted in Chapter 4, as well as the dramatic decline of structured argument more generally, suggest that the rhetorical presidency also marks an increasing inability of governors and governed alike to talk intelligently about the basic principles that define the regime. This was evident in the confirmation hearings for Justices Rhenquist and Scalia where senators serving on the Judiciary Committee failed to probe or question the nominees' constitutional understandings. Senators were comfortable with arguments regarding the presence or absence of political scandal but were unable to sustain any line of questioning of constitutional principle. As the materials in Chapters 2 and 3 indicate, constitutional talk was once commonplace in political debate. It is now the special preserve of judges and law professors, where it is confined to litigational matters. And even at the sanctuary of the Constitution, the Supreme Court, we find justices increasingly willing, perhaps needing, to go public to counter the rhetorical campaigns against them by the president and his attorney general. Has the rhetorical presidency now given birth to a rhetorical judiciary?

I must note again that these examples of systemic costs inhering in, or revealed by, the rhetorical presidency are parts of dilemmas. It

---

Power (New York: Harper and Row, 1972); Arthur G. Theoharis, ''The Rhetoric of Politics: Foreign Policy, Internal Security, and Domestic Politics in the Truman Era, 1945–1950,'' in *Politics and Policies of the Truman Administration*, ed. Barton Bernstein (Chicago: Quadrangle Books, 1970). Kernell concludes, ''Dramatic events may be able to generate a national phobia, but presidential rhetoric cannot'' (*Going Public*, 168).

[10] See Zarefsky, *President Johnson's War on Poverty* (University: University of Alabama Press, 1986), on how Johnson's war on poverty rhetoric shaped the implementation and future discussion of social policy.

is desirable for a polity occasionally to admit of change on the scale of the New Deal; economic recovery, for example, may benefit more from a synoptic vision composed of faulty parts than from a set of well-deliberated but incremental policies. "Energy" has its merits, and popular leadership is sometimes essential to energetic leadership. If political scientists and journalists often err in regarding popular leadership as unequivocably good, one must take care not to assert that the rhetorical presidency is unequivocably bad.

The rhetorical presidency is, equivocably, both good and bad. It is in this ambivalence that one discerns some of the key dilemmas of governance in contemporary America. Yet this ambivalence does not imply a perfect symmetry of costs and benefits. The rhetorical presidency is more deleterious than beneficial to American politics because the rhetorical presidency is not just the use of popular leadership, but rather the routine appeal to public opinion.

Popular leadership seemed necessary and suitable for presidents who faced crises as profound as World War II and the Great Depression. The continual or routine use of the "crisis tool" of popular leadership was meant to make the president more effective in normal times as well. The long-term consequence of the rhetorical presidency may be to make presidents less capable of leadership at any time. If crisis politics are now routine, we may be losing the ability as a people to distinguish genuine from spurious crises. Intended to ameliorate crises, the rhetorical presidency is now the creator of crises, or pseudo-crises.[11] How to harness the rhetorical presidency to the tasks of crisis politics for which it might be essential without adopting it as the routine for all time is the central dilemma.

Campaigns, Wordsmiths, Media

Problems of modern governance are revealed by the theories that produced them, the old and new ways. The potential for energy

[11] Garry Wills, *The Kennedy Imprisonment: A Meditation on Power* (Boston: Little, Brown & Co., 1982); Murray Edelman, *Political Language: Words that Succeed and Policies that Fail* (New York: Academic Press, 1977), 43–49.

through direct appeal or enervation through rhetoric's routinization; the possibility of synoptic change but the danger of legal mutability, substantial political reform but undeliberative politics; and political discourse that is more determinative of, but less reflective about, public policy—all are dilemmas born of that political hybrid that is American politics.

Developments in American politics other than the rise of the rhetorical presidency reflect and reinforce these dilemmas and systemic consequences. Changes in the presidential selection system, the institutionalization of the White House speechwriting staff, and the development of the mass media all contribute to the blessings and burdens of rhetorical governance. These developments did not create the rhetorical presidency—doctrine did—but they have facilitated it. Their importance in American politics is far greater than this, as students of the party system and the mass media have demonstrated, but for present purposes it is sufficient to draw upon the good work on parties and the media, and upon interviews with speechwriters from seven administrations, to indicate briefly how these auxiliary institutions reinforce the best and worst tendencies of the rhetorical presidency.[12]

Campaigns

The roots of the modern campaign-centered selection process go back to Wilson and the Progressives and to many of the same ideas that helped to create the rhetorical presidency.[13] Wilson was the first victorious presidential candidate to have engaged in a full-scale speaking tour during the campaign. His campaign was the first of the now normal "outside" strategies that attempt to form a party around

[12] For a more detailed account of these issues, see James Ceaser, Glen E. Thurow, Jeffrey Tulis, and Joseph M. Bessette, "The Rise of the Rhetorical Presidency," in *Rethinking the Presidency*, ed. Thomas E. Cronin (Boston: Little, Brown & Co., 1982).

[13] See especially James W. Ceaser, *Presidential Selection: Theory and Development* (Princeton, N.J.: Princeton University Press, 1979), ch. 4.

a candidate, rather than to capture nomination by successful appeal to party leaders inside a pre-existing organization. Since Wilson's time, the selection process has become increasingly more "plebiscitary" as primaries have replaced caucuses and state conventions as the means of securing delegates.[14] In Wilson's view, the rhetorical campaign was intended not only to downgrade the role of parties in the selection process, but to prepare the people for a new kind of governance—the rhetorical presidency.

Today the campaign of an incumbent for reelection begins less than two years into his term; challengers begin their campaigns earlier still. The overlap of the electoral campaign with the process of governing means that the distinction between campaigning and governing is being effaced. In the nineteenth century, the tone of campaigns was set by that of governance. Candidates did not issue statements in their own behalf, much less give speeches.[15] By feigning disinterest, candidates exemplified a public teaching that political campaigns were beneath the dignity of men suited for governance, that honor attended more important activities than campaigns. Today, in a striking reversal, campaigns are becoming the model for governing. It is increasingly the case that a president's most important governmental advisers will be those who managed his electoral strategy. Since that strategy is increasingly rhetorical, the skills imported into the White House are more and more those needed to fashion popular appeals. Among top presidential aides likely to be found in any modern administration are advertising executives, pollsters,

[14] See Anthony King, "How Not to Select Presidential Candidates: A View from Europe," in *The American Election of 1980*, ed. Austin Ranney (Washington, D.C.: American Enterprise Institute, 1981), 303–328; Nelson W. Polsby, *Consequences of Party Reform* (New York: Oxford University Press, 1983); and James W. Ceaser, *Reforming the Reforms* (Cambridge, Mass.: Ballinger, 1983). Partly in response to critiques of the primary system like these, recent reforms have moved *slightly* toward a less plebiscitary arrangement. The legitimacy of these new "reforms," in turn, was attacked by Jesse Jackson, who urges us to stay the Wilsonian course.

[15] John Sullivan, "Indecorous Argument: The Use of Madison and Monroe in the Election of 1828," *Southern Speech Communication Journal* 45 (Summer 1980): 378–93.

and polemicists. Both the president and his staff may think of their election as their finest hour, to the extent that its techniques become internalized in their conception of governing. As pollster Pat Cadell advised President Carter at the beginning of his term, "Governing with public approval requires a continuing political campaign."[16]

A growing number of scholars have taken an interest in the selection system with a view toward reform. One defender of the current system recommends it as a proving ground for the very skills necessary to govern well, a rhetorical fitness test.[17] So the modern selection system mirrors the ambivalence of the rhetorical presidency itself. To the extent that this kind of rhetorical leadership is good or necessary, the modern selection system helps to elicit it. To the extent that rhetorical leadership is deleterious, the current selection process makes it worse.

Wordsmiths

The demands of the rhetorical presidency have heightened the importance of speechwriters and expanded their number in recent administrations. Ghostwriting for presidents is not new. George Washington, for example, employed Madison and Hamilton and others in this capacity. The key change is the employment of a group of speechwriting specialists—wordsmiths, as they refer to themselves.[18] This cadre of men and women is a group whose avowed talent is to translate the political policies of others into persuasive prose. They need not have, and increasingly do not have, substantive expertise, but they do sometimes specialize in various aspects of persuasion—partisan attacks, more diplomatic speeches, or comedy,

[16] Patrick H. Cadell, "Initial Working Paper on Political Strategy," mimeographed, December 10, 1979.

[17] Stephen Hess, *The Presidential Campaign* (Washington, D.C.: The Brookings Institution, 1975).

[18] Compare Harry McPherson, *A Political Education* (Boston: Little, Brown & Co., 1972) with James Fallows, "The Passionless Presidency," *The Atlantic* 239 (January 1979): 33–47.

for example. President Carter hired a dramatist to help him develop his speaking technique.

This staff has given the president the ability to respond to events quickly, and to produce speeches, articles, proclamations, press releases, "talking points," "croakers" (eulogies), and assorted other messages in astonishing number. Working in concert with other staffers, especially pollsters, the White House bureaucracy has given the president an increased ability to assess public opinion and to manipulate it.

This staff has at the same time exacerbated the problem of routinization. Many speeches are scheduled long before they are to be delivered. Thus the commitment to speak precedes the knowledge of any issue to speak about, often causing staff to find or create an issue for the speech.

The speechwriting shop has become an institutional locus of policymaking in the White House, not merely an annex to policymaking. To the extent that the imperatives of rhetoric structure policy, the speechwriting staff plays an increasingly central role in the making of policy in the White House as they serve as brokers between policymakers trading phrases. This can be especially important in foreign policy speeches. Members of Carter's staff report that they arbitrated disputes between Secretary of State Cyrus Vance and National Security Advisor Zbigniew Brzezinski. James Fallows reports that, as head speechwriter, he was implored to work out the contradictions in foreign policy articulated in different drafts of a speech prepared by Vance and Brzezinski. Fallows reports that Carter had come to believe that such differences could be reconciled by the rhetorical arts. After Fallows repeatedly insisted that they could not, the president stapled the drafts together and delivered the speech. If Carter could sincerely assert that his foreign policy was coherent, perhaps it would become so, by alteration of the meaning of coherence itself.[19]

The danger here is not, as some suggest, that anonymous speech-

[19] James Fallows, "The Passionless Presidency," *The Atlantic* 243 (May 1979): 33–46.

writers make policy in the name of the president without his knowledge. The very fact that the president has to give the speech insures that he will know what is in it. Speechwriters do not pose a problem of accountability. The problem is rather that by reinforcing the fictive qualities of presidential speech, this institution of experts exercises a subtle but considerable influence upon how a president thinks about politics—upon the presidential mind.[20]

Media

The modern mass media has facilitated the development of the rhetorical presidency by giving the president the means to communicate directly and instantaneously to a large national audience, and by reinforcing the shift from written message to verbal dramatic performance. Major addresses are generally televised, and others are excerpted on the evening news. No other institution or personality is given as much attention by television or newspapers. In the nineteenth century, on the other hand, newspaper coverage of Congress exceeded that of the president.[21]

Yet the history of presidential press relations reveals a progression toward ever less control of the process by presidents. When Teddy Roosevelt first invited reporters into the White House, background and off-the-record rules were clearly articulated and carefully adhered to. Gradually restrictions have lessened and the press has emerged as an autonomous institution, as much a rival and impediment to as facilitator of presidential initiatives.[22]

[20] Speechwriters interviewed from seven administrations included: John Coyne, James Fallows, David Gergen, Hedrick Herzberg, Stephen Hess, and Christopher Matthews. My thanks to them and others who wished to remain anonymous for their insights and observations.

[21] Elmer Cornwell, "Presidential News: The Expanding Public Image," *Journalism Quarterly* 36 (Summer 1959): 275–83.

[22] Elmer Cornwell, *Presidential Leadership of Public Opinion* (Bloomington: Indiana University Press, 1965); James E. Pollard, *The Presidents and the Press* (New York: Macmillan, 1947); Michael B. Grossman and Martha J. Kumar, *Portraying the President* (Baltimore: Johns Hopkins University Press, 1981); Doris Graber, *Mass Media and American Politics*, 2nd ed. (Washington, D.C.: CQ Press, 1984).

The rise of the press as an autonomous institution is important not only for the shift in power that it signifies, but also as a cause of change in the character of presidential speech and of constitutional rule more generally.[23] Speechwriters report that the one-sentence paragraphs so common to presidential messages are consciously designed to accommodate television news. With short aphorisms rather than developed arguments, presidents are more likely to get a snappy quotation on the brief segments of the evening news, and are less likely to be quoted out of context, because there is no context. The regular routine of the news structures the presentation of presidential policy, as presidents time announcements to appear, or not appear, on the evening news. More significantly, presidents now need to attend to the entire set of expected news stories when constructing a speech or announcement, because the whole package of stories creates the context in which president's speeches will be presented and understood.

More profound is the effect of the mass media upon the character of constitutional rule. Television news not only carries the messages of governing officials to the people; it also selects issues to present to the government for action of some sort. ''Real'' expressions of mass opinion, which in the past were sporadically expressed in protest and petition, are replaced by the news's continual sophisticated analyses that serve as a surrogate public. These analyses sometimes include results of public opinion polls commissioned by news organizations. As Harvey Mansfield, Jr. argues, ''surveys are at odds with the idea of representative government as it appears in *The Federalist*: representative government attempts by popular authorization to create scope to govern; surveys have the effect (if not the intent) of closing this space. Surveys create pressure on governments to produce immediate results, sooner even than the next election.''[24] The media's

[23] For an analysis of the power shift, see David L. Paletz and Robert M. Entman, *Media, Power, Politics* (New York: Free Press, 1981), ch. 4.

[24] Harvey C. Mansfield, Jr., ''Social Science and the Constitution,'' in *Political Thought and the Constitution*, ed. Allan Bloom (Washington, D.C.: American En-

use of surveys also influences the way politics is discussed and debated. They reinforce the tendencies induced by the rhetorical presidency to reduce political debate to assertions of policy stands, focusing attention upon what sides citizens take, and how many of them take them, rather than on the complexities of what they stand for. Surveys encourage the polity to jump to the "bottom line" of political argument before deliberation or a genuine political crisis have given citizens reason to be there.

A number of students of the media have shown how the need to present news in a fashion suitable to gain and retain audiences structures the kinds of items reported and the way they are described. Developing its own fictions, even in its presentation of hard news, the media enters political debate and sometimes forces presidential response as each institution vies for control of a world of words. For example, much as President Reagan wishes to describe his anti-missile defense program as "the strategic defense initiative," the media forces discussion of the program as "Star Wars" and holds the president to expectations generated by the movie metaphor.

Constitutional government, which was established in contradistinction to government by assembly, now has become a kind of government by assembly without a genuine assembling of the people. In this fictive assembly, television speaks to the president in metaphors expressive of the "opinions" of a fictive people, and the president responds to the demands and moods created by the media with rhetoric designed to manipulate popular passions rather than to engage citizens in political debate.

Clearly, the modern mass media provides presidents the means to speak to millions of people throughout the world, giving them considerable aid to accomplish the worthwhile needs and purposes of the rhetorical presidency. And there is considerable truth to a keynote of the press's defense of itself: that it is an essential aid to legislative oversight, by uncovering policies in need of defense and by forcing presidents to defend them. Reflecting the ambivalence of popular

terprise Institute, forthcoming). See also idem, "The Media World and Democratic Representation," *Government and Opposition* 14 (Summer 1979): 35–45.

leadership the media also makes it more difficult, in some ways, for presidents to manipulate public opinion, while it reinforces the tendencies of the rhetorical presidency to undermine the possibility of deliberation.

RONALD REAGAN, THE GREAT COMMUNICATOR

In Ronald Reagan, America found the rhetorical president. In the conduct of his administration, we can find the dilemmas of governance in modern America.

Among the consequences of Reagan's election to the presidency was the rewriting of textbooks on American government. It was no longer possible to maintain that interest groups, subgovernments, the checks and balances system, iron triangles, and a demoralized public would frustrate the efforts of any president to accomplish substantial policy objectives, to maintain popularity, and to avoid blame for activities beyond his control.[25]

At the time of the midterm elections in 1986, Reagan could boast of major legislative victories (budget cuts, tax reform, militarization), foreign policy victories (Grenada, the Philippines), substantial changes in the management of the bureaucracy (more centralized control, regulatory reform), a reinspiriting of the population, and a landslide reelection. Most importantly, Reagan's victories on domestic policy were substantial enough to signal a political realignment, although not a shift in party identification as that notion is usually understood. The Reagan realignment is rather a deeper shift in what the parties stand for, in the conspectus of legitimate public policy, and in some institutional arrangements designed to perpetuate these policy shifts (for example, the destruction of the Office of Economic Opportunity on one hand, and massive numbers of judicial appointments on the other). Democrats now talk like Republicans.[26]

[25] For a fine statement of the old wisdom, see Anthony King, ed., *The New American Political System* (Washington, D.C.: American Enterprise Institute, 1977).

[26] For a superb discussion of the Reagan presidency as a realignment in the senses

If these dramatic results reminded us of the powerful potential of the rhetorical presidency, the political scandal that followed the discovery of weapons payments from Iran to Nicaragua forced political observers to reconsider their enthusiasm for it. How could the president not know what was going on in his National Security Council? Journalists dusted off, rewrote, rethought, and republished old stories of how the president of the United States spends his day. A story usually suitable for the Sunday supplement during a slow week suddenly was of acute political interest.

The credibility of Reagan's policies was shaken by the credibility of his insistence not to know what they were. *Time* interviewed White House staffers and the president himself. They discovered a president who often spent more of his day in photo opportunities and greeting dignitaries than in policy discussion, a president who rarely called staffers to probe or elaborate upon their very brief memos to him, a president who allegedly prepared for the Iceland summit by reading a novel.

> Only when it comes to his speeches is Reagan truly a hands-on President. His writers supply the substance; he adds the homespun parables. His attention to speeches reflects his own perception of the job: on many issues he sees himself less as an originator of policy than as the chief marketer of it.[27]

The continual attempts to mobilize the public through the use of personal or charismatic power delegitimizes constitutional or normal authority. Garry Wills noted this phenomenon in the administration of John Kennedy, a president committed to the welfare state. Attempting to pit public opinion against his own government, Kennedy developed a ''counter-insurgency'' style of domestic leadership that paralleled his adventures abroad. Under charismatic rule, order in-

---

I mean, see John Chubb and Paul Peterson, eds., *The New Direction in American Politics* (Washington, D.C.: Brookings Institution, 1985). See also Lester M. Salamon and Michael S. Lund, eds., *The Reagan Presidency and the Governing of America* (Washington, D.C.: Urban Institute Press, 1984), and Fred I. Greenstein, ed., *The Reagan Presidency: An Early Appraisal* (Baltimore: Johns Hopkins University Press, 1982).

[27] ''How Reagan Stays Out of Touch,'' *Time* (December 8, 1986): 34.

heres in the leader, not in the routines of governance. Kennedy aide Theodore Sorenson described some of the institutional consequences of his president's personal presidency:

> [Kennedy] ignored Eisenhower's farewell recommendation to create a First Secretary of the Government to oversee all foreign affairs agencies. He abandoned the practice of the Cabinet's and the National Security Council's making group decisions like corporate boards of directors. He abolished the practice of White House staff meetings and weekly Cabinet meetings. He abolished the pyramid structure of the White House staff. . . .

Successors to a charismatic leader inherit "a delegitimated set of procedures" and are themselves compelled "to go outside of procedures—further delegitimating the very office they [hold]." The routinization of crisis, endemic to the rhetorical presidency, is accompanied by attempted repetitions of charisma.[28] In Reagan's case this cycle was further reinforced by an ideology and a rhetoric opposed to the Washington establishment, to bureaucrats and bureaucracies. "In the present crisis," Reagan said at his Inauguration, "government is not the solution to our problem; government *is* the problem."

One must note that Reagan and his advisers have been sensitive to some of the pitfalls of the rhetorical presidency that I have mentioned. This administration has given considerable attention to the structure of speeches, crafting them not just for the immediate presentation but as written documents as well. While systematic research has not yet been done on the (currently incomplete) Reagan corpus of speeches, preliminary study indicates that a substantial number of those speeches contain an ordered argument and relatively few, compared to the most recent presidents, are mere laundry lists of points. The number of references to the Constitution is also substantial (although many of them also illustrate the warning I made that one not assume intelligent constitutional positions by virtue of the mere invocation of the word). Press conferences have become

[28] H. H. Gerth and C. Wright Mills, eds., *From Max Weber* (New York: Oxford University Press, 1958), 247–48. Garry Wills, *The Kennedy Imprisonment* (Boston: Little, Brown & Co., 1982), ch. 13.

more formalized, with the president regaining substantial control over them. Taken together, these sorts of reforms were intended to recover some of the authority inherent in the office, to contribute to the deliberative process, and to raise important constitutional concerns.

If these developments signal an attempt to attenuate some of the dilemmas of rhetorical leadership, Reagan's love of the movie line and the offhand remark have exacerbated other problems. Under the auspices of the Wilsonian constitution, the "new way," everything a president says is "official." No president has made as much policy as Reagan has on the run, about to board a helicopter, plane, or limousine. At a conference of former White House chiefs of staff, this was noted as a very serious problem. President Carter's chief, Jack Watson, told this story about Reagan's predecessor:

> [President Carter] gave a speech in Washington, just one of those run-of-the mill noonday speeches, and after the speech was over, someone from the press asked him what his attitude about the Mariel boatlift was. It was early in the boatlift. I had cautioned him about saying anything which would give any indication of U.S. approval, but he said something to the general effect that we had a humanitarian duty, we could not let these people die in the ninety miles between Cuba and here, and while they were breaking the law, nevertheless, our government would do everything to save their lives.
>
> That caused tremendous problems because it was interpreted . . . as being an open-door policy. . . . It ended up with our having about 130,000 illegal immigrants cross those Florida Straits.
>
> . . . An offhand remark by the president of the United States frequently can have implications or reverberations of a major decision, as I think that one did.[29]

Journalists had a field day displaying the contradictions in Reagan's account of the Iran policy as he made numerous conflicting statements to reporters in formal and informal settings and as others

[29] Samuel Kernell and Samuel L. Popkin, eds., *Chief of Staff: Twenty Five Years of Managing the Presidency* (Berkeley: University of California Press, 1986), 26–27.

in his administration did the same.[30] It is important to note that the problem of credibility that is induced by such remarks does not necessarily, or solely, derive from a defect of character in the president, but rather is an inevitable byproduct of the institutional context in which modern presidents govern.

The Great Communicator embodies the ambivalence of the rhetorical presidency. A brief review of three major policy campaigns that Reagan considers successes—tax reform, the budget victory of 1981, and the Strategic Defense Initiative—will illustrate this ambivalence more clearly. These policy campaigns each recapitulate the formal qualities of the exemplary cases I discussed in Chapters 4 and 6. Tax reform mirrors the Hepburn Act victory; the budget cuts of 1981 mirror the War on Poverty; and SDI mirrors the League of Nations campaign.

Tax Reform

Among the features of Teddy Roosevelt's success that marked the Hepburn Act as exceptional were: a principled rhetoric that set the agenda of debate without intruding upon the deliberative process; an issue that raised regime-level, constitutive questions; symbolic qualities of the issue that attracted public attention and fueled public concern; skill in coordinating private tactics with public strategy; and exceptional statesmanship within the Congress.

As with the Hepburn Act, few journalists and politicians thought passage of tax reform was possible. However, unlike railroad regulation, its potential failure did not summon fears of a potential Civil War. The issue did not dominate all others as did railroad regulation at the turn of the century. Yet the issue did occupy a central position in Reagan's political agenda. It was the first issue mentioned in his 1985 Inaugural Address, and in his State of the Union Address a month later. He introduced his tax plan in May in a prime-time television address, and he then engaged in several trips around the coun-

---

[30] See, for example, Robert Pear, "Conflicts Abound in Officials Accounts," *The New York Times*, December 4, 1986, p. 16.

try to campaign for the legislation. At crucial junctures, but only at the behest of supporters from both parties, the president, like Roosevelt before him, entered the deliberative process. Much like Roosevelt on judicial review of regulation, Reagan timed his support of various versions of the legislation to "keep the process moving." On a dramatic personal trip to Capitol Hill, Reagan convinced fellow Republicans in the House to support a bill that they did not favor in order to get one that they approved out of the Senate by promising them that he would veto any final bill that did not overcome their most substantial objections.

Reagan's campaign, directed by Secretary of the Treasury James Baker, carefully coordinated the development of draft legislation by the Treasury with simultaneous deliberations on the Hill. From the beginning there was bipartisan interest in the bill. The skepticism that any such a bill could pass was due to the very factor that made possible a good bill. Tax reform had been a continuing subject of discussion on the Hill for decades, and the intense preoccupation of several legislators, such as Senator Bill Bradley, for several years. On the House side, Congressman Dan Rostenkowski combined substantive expertise with an exceptional ability to bargain in a way that did not compromise principle. Indeed, sometimes bargains improved the substantive merits of the bill, as for example the deal to retain IRA deductions for the middle class, but eliminate them for the rich. These extensive hearings were even more thorough than they appeared, since they built upon years of deliberation on the subject.

Political observers were skeptical that tax reform could pass because it seemed to exemplify the very properties that make "collective goods" difficult to realize in our individualistic, interest-based political system. The thousands of provisions of the tax code that would be altered represented the fruits of lobbying of thousands of interest groups who would campaign to preserve their benefits. At the same time, the concrete economic benefit to individuals was projected to be relatively small. Certainly it was perceived to be small, as numerous public opinion polls revealed that most citizens thought that the tax bill would not help them personally, and a majority even believed that the economy as a whole would not be much improved by it. What was in it for the masses?

Reagan's statesmanship was based on the insight that tax reform, despite the economic arguments that informed its legislation, was not fundamentally an economic reform. Rather, it was a political reform that concretely and dramatically raised the issue of the meaning and status of *fairness* and *law-abidingness* in American politics.

The day after passage of the tax reform bill, one of the leading sponsors, Senator Bob Packwood, told the press, "This bill is not about economics, it's about fairness." This echoed the theme that the Republican president had articulated two years previously in his 1984 State of the Union Address, where he had directed his then-Treasury Secretary Donald Regan to develop a plan "to simplify the entire tax code so all taxpayers, big and small, are treated fairly." Fairness was connected to law-abidingness because the unfairness of the code stemmed, in large measure, from complications and loopholes that made evasion both easy and common. The tax code served as a nice metaphor for the integrity of the legal system as a whole, as well as an objective indicator of the law-abidingness of the American people.

When Alexander Hamilton, in *The Federalist*, made a proposal to ensure, and an argument to defend, the sovereignty of the national government, he concentrated upon the power of taxation. This was because the very essence of government, he contended, was coercive authority over individuals. The central defect of the previous "government" under the Articles of Confederation was that it was not a government in fact, only in name, because the states mediated the relation between the national institutions and the individual. Taxation reveals government's primordial power. Under the Articles, only the states were true governments. Under the Constitution, that defect would be remedied.[31] I mention this familiar argument from the *Federalist* to highlight the parallel between the Hepburn Act and tax reform as vessels for regime-level debate.

[31] *Federalist*, nos. 15, 16, 30.

It is in regime-level dispute that the rhetorical presidency is most needed, and happily, it is there that it is most likely to be successful. Success is not guaranteed, of course. Oratorical skill, well-timed and principled (and not-so-principled) bargains, coordination with congressional leaders, media attention, and other contingencies (such as the other current problems facing the nation) all affect the likelihood that one will succeed. It also remains possible for a president to exploit conditions like these to secure a policy to his liking but to the detriment of the regime. Nevertheless, it is in cases like this one that the promise and the noble possibility of the rhetorical presidency display themselves.

The Budget Victory of 1981

As with Lyndon Johnson and his War on Poverty, Reagan's first substantial political victory as president came quickly, drawing upon the "capital" of popularity following his election. Reagan's campaign, like Johnson's, combined exaggerated rhetorical claims and skillful preemption of the deliberative process by avoidance or reconstruction of the rules of legislative debate, with an unstated appeal to public sympathy.

Johnson's victory benefited from the fellow-feeling generated by the national mourning for an assassinated president. Reagan benefited from the sympathy generated by his own near-assassination. He recovered from the poorest approve-to-disapprove ratio recorded by the Gallup poll for any president's second month in office, which had followed his initial televised announcement of plans for many billions of dollars of tax cuts and governmental spending cuts.

Instead of a War on Poverty, Reagan provided a characterization of the economy as "the worst economic mess since the great depression," along with a fantastic diagnosis and prescription of the problem drawn from a school of economics known as "supply side." I call the theory fantastic because Reagan refused to alter it in the face of repeated claims by almost all economists, including many members of his administration, that there was little evidence to support his theory or the particular projections that he made on the basis of it.

Reagan's theory did not so much structure congressional debate as supplant it. Reagan's Office of Management and Budget Director David Stockman figured out a way to subvert a parliamentary measure, known as the reconciliation procedure, that Congress had devised to give itself a greater role in the construction of the federal budget. Reagan skillfully made that procedure an instrument of presidential policy. After a dramatic speech to a joint session of Congress, Reagan won a substantial victory on a general budget resolution. When Rules Committee Democrats tried to force votes on specific appropriations contained in the authorizing resolution, Reagan lobbied on television and on the phone to secure a single up or down vote; and he succeeded, winning in the House 232 to 193. Kernell reports the reaction of Majority Leader James Wright, who "complained bitterly that the administration was trying to 'dictate every last scintilla, every last phrase' of legislation."[32]

Reagan not only tried to dictate the details of legislation, he succeeded. The legislation effectively gutted all the Great Society programs inherited from Johnson's rhetorical presidency fifteen years earlier. Like Johnson's, this massive public policy was prepared hastily in the executive branch, and like the War on Poverty, the nation's legislature played no substantive role in planning the program. In short, there was no public deliberation. Finally, like Johnson's rhetorical campaign, this one created the terms by which the policy would later be held to account and the terms on which subsequent debate would proceed. Later in the term, Reagan achieved substantial tax cuts, but he also became saddled, contrary to the projections of his theory, with the largest national debt in American history.[33]

Star Wars

At the conclusion of the First World War, President Woodrow Wilson attempted to secure peace for generations to come through

[32] Kernell, *Going Public*, 118.

[33] Paul Peterson argues convincingly that the debt problem effectively begins with these policies. Despite decades of Republican rhetoric against the debt, truly massive debt begins with Reagan. Chubb and Peterson, *The New Direction*.

the construction of a new form of political organization, a League of Nations. As I indicated in Chapter 6, Wilson found himself making different arguments to the Senate than he did to the people at large due to different rhetorical imperatives and due to the nature of the issue. To found this precarious possibility he had to elicit enthusiasm for it. To do that, he needed to pretend publicly that the project was not as precarious as he knew it to be.

President Reagan now has the same dilemma although, unlike Wilson, it does not appear that he knows that the Strategic Defense Initiative is a policy fashioned out of rhetorical contradiction. On March 23, 1983, Reagan addressed the nation on television.

> The subject I want to discuss with you, peace and national security, is both timely and important. Timely, because I've reached a decision which offers hope for our children in the 21st century, a decision I'll tell you about in a few moments. And important because there's a very big decision that you must make for yourselves.[34]

The president goes on for most of the speech to defend with some detail and care his pending defense budget. The last thousand words are devoted to the president's "timely" decision, the Strategic Defense Initiative. One would therefore think that the people's "big decision" was to support the defense budget. But clearly the defense budget is the timely matter, while the SDI is the big one. As one proceeds to the end of the speech it appears that the people's decision and the president's are one and the same, to think in a completely new way about strategic defense. Says Reagan:

> . . . I've become more and more deeply convinced that the human spirit must be capable of rising above dealing with other nations and human beings by threatening their existence. . . .
>
> What if a free people could live secure in the knowledge that their security did not rest upon the threat of instant U.S. retaliation to deter a Soviet attack, that we could intercept and destroy strategic ballistic missiles before they reached our own soil or that of our allies? . . .
>
> And as we proceed, we must remain constant in preserving the nu-

[34] Ronald Reagan, "Address to the Nation," March 23, 1983, in *Current Policy* no. 472, Bureau of Public Affairs, U.S. Department of State.

clear deterrent and maintaining a solid capability for flexible response.
. . .

I clearly recognize that defensive systems have their limitations and raise certain problems and ambiguities. If paired with offensive systems, they can be viewed as fostering an aggressive policy; and no one wants that. But with these considerations in mind, I call upon the scientific community in our country, those who gave us nuclear weapons, to turn their great talents now to the cause of mankind and world peace, to give us the means of rendering these nuclear weapons impotent and obsolete. . . .

My fellow Americans, tonight we're launching an effort which holds the promise of changing the course of human history.

This is the program that has come to be known as "Star Wars." The media gave the program the appellation, and it has stuck because it seems to capture the idea of Reagan's speech better than "SDI" does. "Star Wars" seems suitable for a policy that sounds more like science fiction than shrewd defense. And indeed, the policy might have first occurred to Reagan in the late 1940s, when he played the character Brass Bancroft in a movie about a U.S. intelligence agent (Brass) whose mission is to recover a secret weapon that America has developed that renders enemy guns impotent.[35]

In Reagan's vision, defensive systems are not a supplement or adjunct to offensive weapons but an intended replacement of them. This is why his speech fostered the view that to be effective they would have to work perfectly, one hundred percent. In subsequent speeches, the president spoke of the possibility of trading technology with the Soviets in his new defensible world. This vision of an irenic future was articulately criticized by most defense experts in the country who were not in, or associated with, the administration.

The president's own strategic advisers did not so much criticize the policy as reinterpret it in a more defensible, and much more technical, manner. In dozens of speeches, Paul Nitze, Kenneth Edelman,

[35] For a discussion of this and other movie plots and scripts that have reappeared in Reagan speeches, see Michael Paul Rogin, *Ronald Reagan, The Movie, and Other Episodes in Political Demonology* (Berkeley, Calif.: University of California Press, 1987).

Secretaries George Shultz and Caspar Weinberger, and others articulated a very different policy than the president's, albeit one that they
publicly claimed to be the same as his.

In the view of the president's advisers, defensive systems were a
means of improving deterrence, not an alternative to it. They were a
means made increasingly necessary by the Soviets' own developments in this area, a factor not mentioned by the president. In this
view, defensive systems could be effective whether or not they were
ultimately capable of providing a fully protective shield for the nation. Paul Nitze put the point this way:

> . . . Let me emphasize that SDI is not designed to produce a regime
> that would replace deterrence but rather to shift its means. Deterrence
> requires that a potential opponent be convinced that the problems,
> risks, and costs of aggression far outweigh the gains he might hope to
> achieve. A popular view of deterrence is that it is almost solely a matter
> of facing an aggressor with high potential costs in the form of the threat
> of devastating nuclear retaliation. Today, there is no available alter-
> native to this means of deterrence, and thus it is the necessary and
> moral course for us to take.
>
> But deterrence can also function effectively if one has the ability to
> deny the attacker the gains he might otherwise hope to realize. It is our
> hope and belief that a deterrent balance based on *a greater contribution*
> by defense would provide a sounder basis for a stable and reliable stra-
> tegic relationship.[36]

Nitze's argument appears to be the official policy shared by the Defense and State departments and the Arms Control and Disarmament
Agency. But it is not the policy that structured debate in the media.
That debate has focused on the policy as enunciated by Reagan in his
initial speech and repeated by him afterward. The congressional debate has been structured by both policies, and each has been used to
criticize the other. Reagan's speech gives support to those who argue
that combined systems are destabilizing, and the Nitze view gives
support to those who find the president's policy utopian.

[36] Paul Nitze, "Address before the North Atlantic Assembly," San Francisco,
Calif., October 15, 1985, in *Current Policy*, no. 751, Bureau of Public Affairs,
U.S. Dept. of State (my emphasis).

200

Like the League case, Star Wars raises the possibility that rhetoric designed to make a complex or technical issue intelligible and appealing to those who are not in a position to understand the "real" policy will come to constitute the policy it was supposed to explain. And again, the problem of presidential credibility might not result so much from a defect in character as from the competing rhetorical contexts in which presidents and their administrations place themselves.

It is worth noting that President Carter faced similar difficulties with his major legislative initiative. His campaign to establish a National Energy Plan failed miserably during his first year in office. Although a large part of Carter's difficulties were due, as Michael Malbin argues, to lack of political and rhetorical skill, the conflicting demands of popular and deliberative rhetoric were also part of the president's problem.[37] To Congress, Carter urged a long-term plan to ensure availability of fuel in the future—to forestall a crisis. In his popular rhetoric, however, Carter attempted to move the public by suggesting that a crisis already existed. "The key to the plan, noted Richard Rovere, was to convince the public that a crisis existed or, at least, was imminent, and that a failure to meet it with a comprehensive policy would invite 'national catastrophe.' "[38]

Possessed of greater rhetorical skill, Reagan was able to establish his program. Senator Sam Nunn, a proponent of a strong defense and of SDI has perceived the potential for long-term failure engendered by this kind of leadership. The president's rhetoric ". . . causes the scientific community to be shooting in a very broad fashion and is very injurious to a sound program. . . . [It is] probably a political plus in the short term. But in the long term, it's a real trap, not for this president, but for the one who has to go before the American people and say, 'Ooops. I realize Reagan said we're going to protect

---

[37] Michael J. Malbin, "Rhetoric and Leadership: A Look Backward at President Carter's Energy Plan," in *Both Ends of the Avenue*, ed. Anthony King (Washington, D.C.: American Enterprise Institute, 1981).

[38] Sanford Weiner and Aaron Wildavsky, "The Prophylactic Presidency," *The Public Interest* (Summer 1978): 8.

Peoria, but now let me tell you why we've got to protect missile fields in Montana.' ''[39]

Finally, the case of Star Wars raises an issue of still greater gravity. Reagan apparently thinks that the program is designed to protect Peoria. He serves as a better illustration than any previous president of the possibility and danger that presidents might come themselves to think in the terms initially designed to persuade those not capable of fully understanding the policy itself. Having reconfigured the political landscape, the rhetorical presidency comes to reconstitute the president's political understanding.

THE RHETORICAL PREROGATIVE

The ambivalence of the rhetorical presidency is a political fact that, by its nature, can never be fully accommodated by institutional arrangements. Rhetorical leadership is a form of executive discretion, or ''prerogative'' as John Locke called it. According to Locke, ''power to act according to discretion, for the public good, without the prescription of the Law, and sometimes even against it, *is* that which is called *prerogative*.''[40] To think of leadership as prerogative is useful because it is comprehensive; so understood, leadership includes both the power to further popular will and the power to counteract it, according to necessity.

It can be readily seen that leadership as prerogative is dangerous. The common liberal sentiment ''a government of laws, not of men'' recognizes the danger and attempts to contend with it through law. Law is necessary to constrain discretion. Locke shows how doubly problematic the common sentiment is, because prerogative is an ineluctable result of law itself. Law cannot completely provide the means for its own interpretation, because all the contingencies cannot be foreseen and laws contradict one another. These common

[39] Quoted in Fred Barnes, ''Flying Nunn,'' *The New Republic* (April 28, 1986), 19.

[40] John Locke, *Two Treatises of Government*, ed. Peter Laslett, 2nd ed. (Cambridge: Cambridge University Press, 1967), 2nd treatise, ch. 14, sec. 160.

problems of legal interpretation invite and require discretion, which in some cases fill in the gaps of law, in others contravene law altogether in pursuit of the law's aims. Prerogative is thus discretion to pursue the public good, a requirement antithetical to law, yet growing out of law.[41]

How does one ensure that such dangerous, though unavoidable, power is used safely? Locke's answer is that the people, incapable of judging the use of power before the fact, are the only ones capable of judging after the fact. The people can retrospectively judge executive power and, in the worst case, revolt.[42]

Rhetorical power is a very special case of executive power because simultaneously it is the means by which an executive can defend the use of force and other executive powers and it is a power itself. Rhetorical power is thus not only a form of "communication," it is also a way of constituting the people to whom it is addressed by furnishing them with the very equipment they need to assess its use— the metaphors, categories, and concepts of political discourse.

The two solutions to the ambivalence of the rhetorical presidency, the old way and the new, were both constitutional in a modern sense. Modern constitutions are arrangements of indirect governance. They create incentives and disincentives to governors and governed rather than, as ancient regimes did, moral systems to guide political life directly. Because the old and new ways are both forms of indirect governance, neither can accommodate the equivocation of the rhetorical presidency. The founders' solution was to proscribe popular rhetoric always, hoping it would still be around if it was needed. Wilson's solution was to prescribe it always, hoping that it would not be abused. Sustenance for the founders' and Wilson's hopes can only be found outside of the constitutional order. It seems that modern constitutional government must always be biased in one direction or the other, because the discretion needed to mediate between the two is itself antithetical to law and regular procedure, the very point of modern rules of law.

[41] Ibid., sec. 159.
[42] Ibid., sec. 168.

Individual presidents may successfully navigate the contradictory currents created by the conjunction of the old and new ways if they find access to an extra-constitutional perspective, a perspective that informs a rhetorical discretion denied by the old and new ways. But it may be impossible for a constitutional theorist, or political reformer, to provide such a perspective by combining the old and new ways into a single, more coherent, constitution if the reformer wishes to remain true to the core of modern constitutionalism—indirect governance. To be sure, reforms that adhere to the constitutional objective of governing indirectly may be improved by rebuilding institutions like political parties and the presidency itself according to principles that aim for more balance between the old and new ways, by creating greater distance for governance without abandoning all democratic innovations. But institutional reforms of the familiar sort can only attenuate the problems of the rhetorical presidency. They cannot face them head-on.

If ancient politics was intrusive because it regulated private affairs, it also permitted, in one sense, greater political freedom, because the polity remained closer to and more aware of its constitutive principles. Political accommodation of the ambivalence of the rhetorical presidency requires a modern equivalent of the ancient scheme, because governors and governed need a theoretical compass with which to position themselves to be able to assess appropriate and inappropriate exercises of power. Citizens of a reformed polity, regulated by such a compass, would be able to judge the rhetorical categories in which power is expressed, defended, and understood. Their presidents could responsibly avail themselves of a political tradition that offers rhetorical exemplars of principle, vision, and silence.

One cannot overestimate the difficulties in conceiving and promoting such a polity. Nevertheless, to provide citizens and presidents with a new political education, more than to tinker with institutional incentives and disincentives, is the fundamental task facing America today. This book is an advertisement, perhaps a preface, for that education.

INDEX

Adams, Henry, 56
Adams, John, 49, 61, 62n, 64, 66, 69–70
Adams, John Quincy, 61, 64, 66, 72–73
addresses. *See* rhetoric
Aldrich, Nelson, 98–100
Alexander, Holmes, 76n
Ames, Fisher, 49, 69
Ammons, Harry, 71n
Aristotle, 32
Arnhart, Larry, 32n
Arrow, Kenneth, 34n
Arthur, Chester A., 64, 66, 85

Bainard, Harry, 84n
Baker, James, 194
Baker, Ray Stannard, 105
Barber, James David, 88n, 90n, 93
Barber, Sotirios A., 8n
bargaining, 10–12, 107
Barnes, Fred, 202n
Bemis, Samuel Flagg, 72
Benedict, Michael Les, 91n
Bessette, Joseph M., 11n, 15n, 38n, 182n
Bibby, John, 162n, 166n, 170n, 172n
Bishop, Joseph B., 99n
Blum, John M., 98n, 99n, 107
Blumenthal, Richard, 162n
Bohlen, Charles, 179n
Bradley, Bill, 194
Brann, Eva T. H., 82n
Bryce, James, 177
Brzezinski, Zbigniew, 185
Buchanan, James, 64, 66, 78–79, 141
budget cuts, 22, 196–97
Butler, Benjamin F., 91n, 92

Cadell, Patrick H., 184n
campaigns, 182–84
Cannon, Joe, 107
Carter, Jimmy, 3, 139, 174–75, 192;
    moral malaise speech, 3, 5n, 136, 141
Ceaser, James W., 9n, 28, 35n, 76n, 96n, 124n, 182n
Chalmers, David M., 98n, 99n, 101n, 105
character, presidential, 21, 93, 131–32, 147–52, 190–91, 202
Chester, Edward W., 50n
Chinard, Gilbert, 70
Chitwood, Oliver Perry, 76n
Chubb, John, 190n
Cicero, 32
Clay, Henry, 177
Cleveland, Grover, 64, 66, 85
Clor, Harry, 119n
comparative leadership, 6n
constitutional order: Anti-Federalists
    on, 26n; constitutive thought, 17–23;
    nineteenth century, 26–45; twentieth
    century, 118–32
Cooper, James Fenimore, 29
Cooper, John Milton, 115n
Cornwell, Elmer, 12n, 106, 107n, 145n, 186n
Corwin, Edward, 8n
credibility problem, 147–61
crisis, 174–81. *See also* prerogative
Cromwell, Oliver, 115
Cronin, Thomas, 10n
Cunningham, Noble E., 56n
Cutler, Lloyd, 44n

Davidson, Roger, 162n, 166n, 170n, 172n

205

Library of Congress Cataloging-in-Publication Data

Tulis, Jeffrey.
The rhetorical presidency.

Includes bibliographical references and index.
1. Presidents—United States—History. 2. Political
oratory—United States—History. I. Title.
JK518.T84 1987   353.03'23   87–45542
ISBN 0–691–07751–7 (alk. paper)